Cheers Mom

Cheers Mom

CHANGE YOUR THINKING, CHANGE YOUR LIFE

Katrina Anderson

Printed in the U.S.A.

Second Printing, 2018.

Print on Demand. Save trees.

ISBN 978-1-9994943-0-8

Published by Katrina Anderson

2808 Donald B. Munro Dr.

Kinburn, Ontario

K0A 2H0

www.kinburnfarms.com

Cover Photo Credit – Gerhard Bögner

Cover Design Credit – pro_ebookcovers

Lotus Flower Credit – GDJ

Dedication

This book is dedicated to everyone that has felt at one point in their life like giving up on going after something they wanted. I hope it inspires you to know you can do anything with the right perspective and a true belief in yourself. You can create a life you love; it all begins with your thoughts.

It is also for those struggling with anxiety or grief. It's okay not to be okay sometimes. I hope through sharing my story you will find the courage to talk about what's going on inside, and know that you are not alone.

Acknowledgement

I would like to thank my Father, Denis MacNeil for all the hours he spent editing and re-editing this book for me. This is very close to home for both of us, and I am so appreciative for his tireless dedication in supporting me throughout this project. A huge thank you to Amy Courtney as well for all the time she spent helping me tweak and improve my wording, so I could say so much more with less.

I would like to thank our children for their patience and understanding while I took the time to write this book. Their love and laughter kept me going, and their smiles and hugs reminded me every day why it was so important for me to finish it.

Most of all I would like to thank my husband for the countless times he would take our kids outside to play and leave me with a quiet house to write, and for all the days he would push me to keep going when I got discouraged. His unending support and love kept me believing in myself throughout not only writing this book, but in all the challenges we have faced together in life.

Table of Contents

Chapter 1

It's Been a While

Hi Mom,

Wow. It feels weird to write that. The only time I write "Mom" now is a signature on a note telling someone what I have left out for supper, or reminding them to shower and wash their butt. Those notes are for the kids obviously, not Chris. It feels good to write it. It feels safe. It feels like home. I wish I could be saying it and not writing it, but hey, that's life.

I can't believe it has been ten years since you left, which from here on in is how I will refer to when you passed away. "Passed" sounds like you're gone for good, "left" sounds like you're still floating around somewhere, which I want to believe. I want to think you're always nearby, to see me, to be proud of me.

You left a hole when you went. It hurts. Everyone told me the pain would never go away but I didn't believe it. Now I know it's true. I'm okay though Mom, please know that. I have so many of your great qualities, the biggest one being your strength. I am truly happy, and I don't think many people can say that. You taught me to embrace life, whatever it brings and I am learning to do just that.

I won't say it has been easy. The first few years were a total blur. I would go through the day – laundry, groceries, dealing with the kids, all with a stupid smile on my face pretending I was managing. At night behind closed doors Chris would hold me and I would quietly cry myself to sleep night after night, year after year. He and the kids were so amazing, keeping me together as best they could.

Two years after you left, when the boys were 3 and 4 we decided to move closer to town. Clayton was great and all, but commuting two hours a day each was definitely wearing on us, and the pocket book. Dad was selling the Farm at the time but there was no way I thought I could live on the Farm again. Turns out after seeing lots of different houses we ended up putting in an offer on a property – the one right across the road from the Farm actually. It passed all inspections, the last condition being that we sold our house first.

It was not to be. We didn't sell our house in Clayton in time to get the financing, and we lost the deal. Of course the very next day our house in Clayton sold. I remember looking up at the sky and saying "Okay Mom, I get it, we'll buy the Farm." Don't know if you heard me but if that was you pulling the strings, thank you. Turns out it was the best thing for us.

We moved in and Dad moved to the round house next door. I love telling people its story, "Remember in playgrounds those metal domes full of triangles that you'd hang upside down from as kids? Well my Grandpa invented that structure and built a house with it in Kanata. Then when he sold the land we put it on a truck and plopped it in Kinburn." I mean, really, how cool is that?

It was great being closer to town and Chris's kids, Kevin and Hannah, and all the kids having all the same fun I did growing up here. It was really hard though Mom, really, really hard to live in your house without you here. Knowing you weren't ever going to come home again, bouncing through the front door with a load of groceries and your beautiful smile. I have so many great memories of how you'd come home and throw the cupboard stuff at me hot potato style, making putting away groceries fun. Our kids love it now too.

Missing you started to wear on me. I needed to throw something in the mix for me to keep my mind busy. The government had this thing where if you submitted a proposal for education, showing how it would further your career, they would pay for it. So I decided to wake up the old hamster in my brain and get her wheel spinning again.

I started taking a "Sustainable Agriculture" course on-line with University of Guelph. It was awesome to be in school again, I love it as much as you did. Long story short, I totally kicked ass and finished with a 98% average. Harriet the hamster was fit as a fiddle apparently.

On the surface I am sure things seemed to be going well. I was doing all I could to keep busy and move on from losing you but I just couldn't move past the grief. The more I tried to ignore it, the more it consumed me. I was drowning in it. One day I couldn't keep it together any more. It was four years after you left.

I was at work, in the bathroom having a wee bubble all to myself, now a daily ritual. I had gotten used to stealing away at lunchtime and releasing the floodgates for a couple of minutes. I remember standing and leaning with my back against the wall and letting the tears fall only this time they wouldn't stop. All of a sudden I couldn't breathe. My heart was so heavy with grief I was suffocating. I slid down along the wall and crumpled into a puddle on the floor. I could feel it coming, it had years of momentum. And that's when it happened.

I had a complete nervous breakdown.

It all came out. I had never felt such an intense release. It lasted only a few minutes, but in that short time I realized I was completely losing my mind and I had to do something.

With not an ounce of energy left, my sleeves covered in snot and my shirt soaked with tears, I went upstairs to see my supervisor. She had been amazing since you passed and I knew she would be discreet and supportive. I went up to her with three words that I had not yet said to anyone, that would change my life.

"I need help."

She held me and said three words as equally important. "Yes, you do."

The next day I found myself sitting on a couch and pouring my heart out to a psychologist. I put down my emotional shield, hung up my Superwoman cape and bawled for ten minutes straight. Then I started talking about it, more openly than I had yet with anyone. It's weird how I could with an absolute stranger but not someone close.

I felt better, better than I had since the day you left. I knew it was the first step in getting my life back, and finding 'me' again. Not the 'me' that I put on for everyone else, but the real me, the happy me. I needed her back, and slowly, and with a lot of work, I found her again, and I am so glad for it.

Dad is doing great, wonderfully really, but it took a long time. He is finally happy I think. He leads a busy life – far more exciting than mine. He is still marshalling in Calabogie during the summers and curling in Pakenham in the winters. The business is still going strong but I think slowly he is stepping back, knowing now it has the right momentum to keep going on with the staff he has in place.

He even bought a motorcycle which he rides all the time – so awesome for a man 71 years young. And don't worry Mom, as promised, I have kept him fed. He comes over every week for Pasta Friday, and has since the day you left.

Our relationship has definitely changed in the last ten years. He has been amazing. He has done everything he could to be whatever I need in the 'parents' department. He is an amazing Grandpa, teaching the kids all kinds of stuff, even about the Romans – yawn. It's kind of funny to watch their eyes glaze over at the very same kitchen table mine used to as they quietly nod and attempt to look interested. I love him so much, even with the history lessons.

We're very close now. We can finally talk about you, just in the last year or two; it was far too tender before. It is still raw, always will be I guess but I am done trying to hide emotionally with him. If the tears well up, I let them fall. I know sometimes he doesn't know what to say, but you know Dad, with one look you can see what his heart is saying, and it is always I love you, and I miss her too. It's the look that says how proud you'd be of me that really touches me. That's all I ever wanted from you guys.

Ryan is doing great too, you raised a wonderful son. His boys are now 11 and 14 and are growing up into fine young men. He is an absolutely fantastic Dad and devotes a ton of his time to bringing his kids here and there for sports and different things. He and I can't talk about you yet and I don't know if we ever will but that is okay. Looks between us say far more than words do too.

Chris and I are as tight as ever, its 16 years this year. His kids are now 18 and 21 and have grown up into amazing young adults, you would be so proud of them. Their Mother and I have become really close over the years; she is truly a good person and an amazing Mother. I'm so glad we all never got into all that crap some people do with their exes, it only ends up hurting the kids, and overall, life is just too damn short. You leaving taught me that.

Our two boys are now 11 and 12 and are turning into really amazing young men. They are compassionate, free-spirited, very kind hearted and chalk full of surprises. I call them our "hayseeds". You'd be so proud of them. I have lots of stories I am going to tell you, but first I'll catch you up on the world's biggest changes in the last ten years.

Reese Peanut butter cups now come in a package of 4 – it's a game changer.

Environmentally the world is going downhill. Climate change and global warming are a real thing, even though lots of people still refuse to recognize it. Glaciers are melting, our waters are polluted, and landfills are overflowing. Slowly but surely though, more and more people are waking up and making better environmental choices.

The local food movement is going strong too, thankfully, as more and more crap is going into our processed foods. I can't even pronounce half of the ingredients in our junk cupboard. We do our best to eat healthy at every meal, but sometimes life gets busy. I ate Kraft dinner now and then as a kid, and I turned out all right, and so will they. Kind of wish I had the passion for cooking that you did but, whatever, I didn't get that gene.

Technologically the internet was around when you were, but it has exploded in ways you can't imagine. It is so mindboggling Mom. You can find absolutely anything on-line now – how to bake an apple cake (yours is still the best), someone popping the world's biggest zit or the population of China. Its bananas, and such an easy way to waste time when you get sucked into something.

Remember the brick of a cell phone you had? Those days are long gone. Now they're as thin as half a deck of cards and are basically mini computers in your pocket. People now can "text" instead of talk on their phones – which is when you send a typed message. It's great to be able to get a quick note to someone without having to interrupt them. I can't count the number of times "milk please" or "good morning lover" have flown between Chris and I.

They now have these funky little symbols called "emoji's" that you can send along with your message. There is one for pretty much anything you can think of – a smiley face, sad face, barfy face – whatever you want. They can be things too – an avocado, a little painter dude, the Canadian flag or my personal favourite – a piece of poo.

Cell phones now can take photos and videos, which is great but also has its downfalls. I remember going to a school play a few years ago and watching this beautiful little girl singing her heart out to her Mom in the front row. All she wanted was her Mom to watch her and be proud. All she could see though was the cell phone in front of her Mom's face as she videoed it. I could see her disappointment, to which the Mother was completely oblivious. It always stuck with me and I remind myself of it when I catch myself doing the same thing.

Parenting has totally changed too. Life was so much less complicated years ago. When I was a kid, you went outside, you played, you got dirty and only came in for meals or if you got broken. Now the internet has scared the crap out of everybody about everything. Germs are bad, dirt is bad, stay safe, don't take risks, don't talk to strangers. It's ridiculous. People are afraid to let their kids do anything – they call it "helicopter parenting".

I am guilty of it too. Chris and the boys are always joking with me that I need a cape stitched with WCSG – Worst Case Scenario Girl. He'll say "What's Mom's call sign guys?" to which they joyfully reply – "Hey, let's have fun." Little devils, but I know they're right, I can be overprotective. It's because I love them so much and can't bear to think of them hurt.

Turns out they have turned into just what we had hoped for – kind, thoughtful, independent out of the box thinkers. So many times we have found them doing something completely crazy that was at the same time absolutely brilliant. You know what I mean, those moments as a parent when you don't know whether to get mad or applaud. I've learned to turn off my chopper and remind myself that if we want to teach them how to pick themselves up we have to let them fall down.

Which brings me to today's 'social media' – a phrase we now use for different platforms (websites) where people share photos and stories, often about how picture perfect their life is – look at my perfect hair, my golden children, my big brand new expensive car. The most popular one is called "Facebook"; I think it was just starting to grow when you left. Then of course there are the real life pics I put up of our hayseeds – grass stained knees, mud fights, and the hole in the wall I found the size of a boy's foot. To his credit, at least he tried to tape it back together before he told me about it. Bless his heart.

It's a great way to see what friends and family have been up to. Speaking of which – everyone is doing great. I don't get a chance to see my cousin on your side as much as I'd like, but she is doing well and her three kids are happy. There are now 24 great grandchildren on Dad's side and ONLY 3 of them are girls! Nana is still rockin' – now 101 years young. Dad visits her every week and she has apparently stopped kicking his butt at crib. Fair enough, her foot must be tired. The whole family got together for her last birthday, as we still all do for Christmas, alternating houses every year.

Every year on the day you left, a bunch of us get together for a dinner out. This year, with it being the 10th anniversary I am going to do something special. I think we'll have it at Dad's and I am going to attempt to make a speech and do my best to get through it. Ten years later Mom, and it still feels like yesterday.

It's weird. It's like if I don't feel sad when I think about you that somehow means I am starting to forget you. I still have those moments when something amazing happens and I go to reach for the phone to call you, or in the morning there is still that split second when all seems right with the world, and then I remember. It's definitely getting easier, and happy memories come floating far more often than the sadness.

I think that this is why I had to write you this letter. To just let some things go. Losing you was the most terrible and gut wrenching thing I have ever gone through in my life, but it also gave me the biggest gift. It taught me to never take anyone for granted. It taught me how precious life is and that in one instant it can change forever. It has made me a better daughter, a better wife, a better Mother but most of all, a better me.

Remember how I was always a worry wart? Well, worrying took over my mind the last part of 2015 and by spring 2016 it was full blown anxiety. Not the kind that makes your palms sweaty and you feel extra nervous, but a feeling that would take over some days so badly I could barely function. Constant panic attacks, throwing up and losing weight was my life. It totally sucked. I mean some days I felt like I was seriously losing my mind. It was so scary Mom. The worst part was, I was too ashamed to ask for help and thought I could get through it alone.

Nobody had any idea. The more pain I felt, the bigger my smile. The more broken I became, the bigger the show I put on for the world. Chris knew about it, but he had no idea really how bad it was, no one did, and no one does to this day. I haven't told anyone the real truth, ever. It was my shameful little secret. I was living in a nightmare I had created myself. It is two years later and it has taken a heck of a lot of work, mostly to realize it is nothing to be embarrassed about. Everybody has crap in their life; it's okay to not be okay sometimes.

About 6 months into it, I finally got the guts to start opening up and sharing honestly what I was going though. I was blown away by how many other people suffer from anxiety too. You never know what is really going on behind someone's smile, everyone that has their silent battles, no matter how 'together' they seem.

Before I dive into what we're doing now, I want to tell you where my head is and how my perspective has changed – with everything. Of course the main lesson came from you long ago, I guess it just took a few more years to really sink in.

I can't always choose what happens in my life, but it is my choice *how to think about it*. I accidentally drop and smash a glass; well at least there were no little bare feet nearby to get cut. A "fluff" as you called them squeaks out while I am lifting something heavy, well at least no one was around to hear it right? There's always a bright side, you just have to learn to train your brain to see it first.

The kids do it automatically now too, I guess after hearing me do it so often. Just yesterday one of them went to grab a bagel but there was none left – "Well, at least there's bread I can have instead." Awesome.

I have spent the last few years studying the power of language, the subconscious mind and neuroplasticity. I get it now Mom, I finally get it. I have the power to be proactive in my every thought, not simply reactive. I make the choice of how to think and see things; I just always have to remember my A, B, C's;

Attitude is everything. Believe in Yourself. Create your Life.

Of course, you were a great example of all three.

The day after you told me you had cancer we went for lunch. You smiled and said, "Everybody says why me? Well, I say why not me? I am as good as anybody else. I'm so lucky to have lived the life I have." I can't think of anyone else that would have looked at it that way. Talk about a great attitude.

I remember your passion working to prevent injuries and save lives on the road. All those trips to Toronto for meetings, all the conference calls and all the late nights, you never lost sight of your goal. Mom you can't imagine how proud I am when I tell people that Graduated Licencing here in Ontario was a seed that you first planted at our kitchen table. You did it, you made it happen because you never gave up and kept believing in yourself.

Right after I had our second baby, you and I were having a heart to heart over a cup of tea on my couch. I was stressing out about making money. You put your hand on my knee and looked me straight in the eye. I'll never forget what you said to me, as you said it with such conviction and love, "Figure out what you love to do, and then find a way to make money doing it."

Looking back, I can see that is how you always lived. You knew the life you wanted to live, and then you created it. No wonder you looked back on your life with such gratitude and no regrets.

I know now Mom that when you have a dream, you don't have to know "how" you'll get there; you just have to know that you will. No matter what comes up for us now, it isn't a question of if we can do it or not, it's more a question of how much of a pain in the butt will it be to do.

Did you know that Colonel Sanders (KFC guy) had his recipe rejected 1009 times before the first restaurant said yes? Or that Walt Disney filed for bankruptcy 7 times before he made it big?

"Think you can or think you can't – either way you'll be right." Henry Ford was a smart man. It's all about never refusing to give up on your dream, not matter how many times you fall before you fly.

So is it driving you nuts yet Mom what we are doing now? Have you figured it out? Well the jig is up, time for the great reveal...

Chapter 2

"It does not matter how slowly you go

as long as you do not stop."

- Confucius

That isn't Yoghurt!

In April of 2011 I was running, I tripped and went down full speed on my right shoulder. Total klutz move, I haven't changed at all Mom. I cracked my collar bone and separated my shoulder. Holy crap did it ever hurt. I was off work for six weeks.

Fast forward to April 2012, exactly one year to the week after I had first wiped out.

I missed a step and flew down the red kitchen staircase as if on roller skates. I threw up my arms to steady myself but it didn't slow me down one bit. Chris was at baseball that night so I had nobody to whine to. I carried on and did the dishes, swept the floor, got the kids to bed, blah blah blah and went to bed myself. I barely slept.

I woke up the next morning in excruciating pain. I looked in the mirror and to my horror my right shoulder was hanging about an inch lower than my left. Crap. Drove to the hospital and found out I had separated it – again. Dummy.

At the same time there were huge layoffs going on in the Government. They had also introduced an "Alternation" program. If someone who had lost their job, found someone still employed who wanted to leave, and they met that person's job qualifications, then they could take over that job and the person could leave with their pension and no penalty.

I liked my job enough at the time, but I wasn't really growing or learning. I had been applying to every job competition for the past two years, but I hadn't gotten anywhere yet. I felt stuck. I don't like feeling stuck.

I had just finished a year at Guelph learning about a great business model for small scale farming. "CSA" – Community Supported Agriculture is where people buy a 'share' in your Farm. It's such a brilliant idea Mom. Basically people commit to buying a certain amount of farm products before they're even grown, so the Farmer knows how much to grow and nothing is wasted.

I had been tossing the idea around in my head of leaving the government and starting farming full–time, but was petrified to make the leap. Chris and I had a "board" meeting at the kitchen table. Did we want to do it? Yes. Did we know how we would do it? No, but we'd *figure it out*.

I have to admit Mom, it was pretty neat to be sitting at the very same table you and Dad did so many times, figuring out which direction to go, and here we were doing the same thing so many years later. I learned watching you and Dad so many times to not get caught up in the "how" you are going to do something, just keep focusing on the "why" and everything will always fall into place. The layoffs gave me the final push I needed. I found someone who was laid off and could take my job. I quit my job a week after my shoulder quit me.

Our vision was to bring back the small scale family Farm. We'd produce all of our own hay and straw, grow veggies and raise all kinds of animals for meats. We'd buy everything – tractor, lumber, hardware, feed, baby oinkers and moos from within 20km. That was our plan. Work with our neighbours and put out a great product. It was exciting and scary all at the same time. Exactly the place I love to be.

So I should let you know now Mom, before I get any further that I'll be telling you crazy stories about raising livestock. Some are pretty gross, and some are just downright hilarious. Many I wouldn't dream of telling anyone else, but it's you I'm talking to. I know you won't judge me, and you'll appreciate our determination.

We hatched out a business plan. In the next two years we would (Chris would) build two more barns, and install all the fencing, electrical, plumbing, gates and whatever else was needed. Chris is so kick–ass Mom. He was signing up for all of this, on top of keeping his full time job. Raising four kids without at least one steady paycheck just wasn't an option. Kids need stuff.

We started 'Kinburn Farms' two weeks after I quit. At the time we only had the old horse barn and a chicken coop we had built the year before. The rest was still just fields for grain and corn. We had a ton of work to do.

We were really excited about what lay ahead. I'm so like you Mom, someone who loves far more the thrill of "what could be" rather than the comfort of staying in "what is". I couldn't wait to start every day. I'd wake up vibrating; often so early I'd have to wait for the sun to come up so I could start working. Now that's passion.

I knew I needed to learn as much as I could. I spent a lot of time those first few weeks visiting other farms with livestock and big gardens. I asked lots and lots of questions. All of the farmers I talked to told me we couldn't do it. It was too hard. One lady nearby who owned a huge commercial vegetable business flat out told me I was making a terrible mistake and I was a fool. I politely thanked her for her time, bit my lip and left. I drove away mumbling to myself "Just Watch Me".

Pretty much everyone else said we were nuts too. When I'd tell people how I had quit my "secure" government job to grow food, they'd look at me like I had six heads. It became clear, pretty quickly that most people saw farming as some kind of lower level profession. Totally ridiculous. Farmers grow food. People need food or they die. Pretty important job if you ask me.

The nicest response I got came from John up at the Farm Supply. We had gotten to know each other a little over the two years since we had bought the Farm. I told him I'd quit my job and what our plans were. "Well, I promise you'll earn every dollar you make." He was right.

I knew one thing for sure from watching you and Dad grow your business as I grew up. If Chris and I always had passion for what we were doing, we'd make it work. It might take way longer than we thought, and probably cost a ton more, but we'd do it. We would live by our values, always do what was right and never give up. No sweat, we've been building stuff since we started dating. You know how well we work together, one of my favourite things about us.

That first month after we started we met a farmer who was retiring. We'd be able to purchase his herd in the fall. 1 bull, 6 pregnant cows, and 6 six month old calves. We signed his dotted line, we would buy his herd. We were now committed. Holy crap. It was really happening.

I was a crazy woman that first month and had lists coming out the Ying Yang – sound familiar? We had a whiteboard in the kitchen (Command Central) to keep us focused and on track. Nothing drives me battier than running in circles, trying to do a million things and accomplishing none. I think that's a Mom thing.

It was so overwhelming with so much to think about – a business plan, bank loans, sourcing everything and making realistic deadlines. I'd have a hard time sleeping because I just I couldn't shut my brain off. I'd wake up all hours of the night, fly out of bed to add to the whiteboard or work on the computer. It felt so damn amazing to be so passionate about something again. I knew I was finally doing what I was meant to do. And the loves of my life were right beside me.

When we started Kinburn Farms, Charles was five and William was four. They could dress themselves, of course with shirts and sometimes pants on backwards but hey, they did it, right? They could play alone but still needed eyes on them, because, well, you know, kids are nuts – especially ours. I always joke about how free range they are and I'm so grateful for it. They have definitely taught us there is always time for silliness and surprises.

The irony was we were working night and day to grow all kinds of healthy food, while behind closed doors we were eating whatever was fastest and easiest.

At first I'd beat myself up for not being the perfect little Suzy homemaker. Then I'd remind myself they'd be fine if they didn't eat kale every day. They'd survive wearing the same shirt two days in a row or if they skipped a bath or three during the week. I just had to remember the most important thing Mom – NEVER run out of ketchup!

Our three main goals for the spring and summer of 2012 were; Market the Farm, Start a Veggie CSA and Bring in Some Livestock.

To start marketing the Farm I set up a Facebook business page. Slowly more and more people "liked" it. That means that what I would post would show up on their 'wall' while they were checking their Facebook account. It was a great way to showcase the values behind our business, as well as what we were selling. True confession, I have since turned into a Facebook junkie. It is SUCH a great way to procrastinate. No wonder the man who invented it is a gazillionaire.

Word slowly got around and more and more people started visiting the farm. It helped on the farm tours that I'm a great story teller just like you, as well as a complete goof. I'd tell them how we'd soon be buying a herd of cattle, even though I hadn't ever even touched a cow. Kind of ridiculous looking back, actually.

The question people asked us most often – Will you be organic? My reply – cow hurts foot, cow can't walk, cow can't get to water, cow dies, or... cow hurts foot, vet comes and gives antibiotics, cow walks again, burgers for everyone. I'd phrase it differently but the point was the same. Turns out 99% of people were looking for exactly what we would be offering, once they knew exactly what it was. Within three weeks we had presold all of our CSA veggie shares and meat chickens for the upcoming season. It felt amazing; our marketing was paying off.

I was also putting up flyers I had made here, there, and everywhere as not everyone's on Facebook. I would work what we were doing into conversations with people I would run into, and even people who were nearby would hear me talk and ask me about it. One day I was telling a friend who owned a kid's consignment store in Kanata about our plans, and the lady in line behind me introduced herself.

Her name was Lisa, and Mom this woman exudes kindness and good. She had 5 kids at the time and was really excited about what we were doing. She told her sister Jaime about us too, and both those wonderful women have been customers ever since, and definitely two of my most favourites. The kind of customers that I don't feel I have to go on and on about our ethics and values, they just get it. They have been with us since the very beginning and I love our chats when they visit, and they give great hugs too.

We put the garden in the same spot you had yours, the one you used to grow those humungous cauliflowers in and sell to Loblaw's all those years ago. I think it's about 40' x 60'. I thought that I had planted enough to fill ten CSA baskets every week with veggies. Wow, was I ever wrong Mom. Oopsie.

I planted all kinds of veggies and then soon started freaking out when I realized there wouldn't be enough. So then I started planting in walkways and every square inch I could. Of course it turned into an absolute nightmare when I'd water. I ended up dragging hoses all over the garden, taking out a ton of seedlings in the process. Great way to make your head explode.

The summer of 2012 was not just a dry year Mom, but a full on drought. The lawn turned into a brown dried coco mat. There was nothing for bugs to eat in the lawn so they saw the garden as their own private buffet. In a few short days they destroyed several rows of veggies. Jerk bugs. Apparently growing organic wasn't so easy. I still loved every minute of it though, regardless. I was learning a ton and was outside growing stuff.

I had to figure something out. No way was I going to quit the garden; I had committed to our customers. I sent an email letting all our veggie customers know I'd be supplementing their CSA basket with organic produce from other local farms. Thankfully everyone was fine with that. Lots of the farms I approached told me their veggies were 'pretty much organic', and 'nobody would know the difference'. But I would and that's all that mattered. You were definitely successful Mom at drilling the importance of integrity into us growing up. I won't do anything that doesn't feel right.

Our well went dry soon after, then three weeks later it went dry again. Crap. I shut down the veggie CSA. All of our customers understood. I'm so glad I didn't follow the standard CSA model and collect the full season's cash up front; people were only paying us weekly. I could have had a pity party; but I realized it couldn't have turned out better really. We now had a lot more time to get the Farm ready for the animals coming soon. Perfect, that was just what we needed.

I remember the day I ordered the baby birds from the Feed store. It was full of errands and by the end the kids were going absolutely bananas. I had lost my cool hours ago, and the feed store was our last stop. They were like little cyclones in the store. John was so good, he said nothing. A father of three himself, he totally understood.

I was giddy like a kid at Christmas the day the birds arrived. They sat peeping away in their boxes, all with air holes on the top of the sides serving as a viewing gallery. In the mayhem the week before, I had accidentally ordered day – olds chicks, not two week – olds. It would be too cold outside for them, they'd have to live in the house for a bit. We of course had nothing ready – so we had to whip something up right quick.

We put the bird boxes in our bedroom and started building their temporary indoor pen downstairs. We could hear the birds peeping away and then two or three playful barks from Stella, who was 2 years old at the time. Then absolute silence. My stomach sank. I ran upstairs to see our bedroom door open and Stella inside looking at me with that "Oh crap, I am really going to get it" look. Did she ever.

It looked like tiny fluffy yellow tennis balls had been thrown all over the bedroom. But no, in actual fact, they were 18 dead baby chicks. I was sick to my stomach. I started shaking. I couldn't believe it Mom. I got a garbage bag and began picking up all the carnage, gagging the whole time. Tears were running down my cheeks. Stella has this great way of being able to open doors, no matter how well they're shut. Great dog, but she can be a real pain in the butt sometimes.

The whole situation woke up TOM (my tiny obnoxious monster). Years ago I decided to give my anxiety a name, to somehow in my head disconnect it from the real me, the 'level headed go getter' me. It gave me someone to tell to shut up.

I imagine he looks a lot like the green goblin guy from Just for Laughs, with evil little beady black eyes. He is definitely a worst case scenario jerk. His taunts always stem from the idea that someone is going to get hurt or dead because of something I did. Those poor baby chicks got hurt – actually dead while in my care. I owned it, and then let it go. Nothing could be changed but I knew what NOT to do next time. Lesson learned, move on.

I ordered a bunch more chicks. The kids had a ball those first couple of weeks they lived inside. I would go in the "bird room" (which now had a lock on it) to find them lying on their bellies, surrounded by wee feathered friends, often one or two on their heads. They don't poop all that often right?

One time I went in to find the kids sitting cross legged without a bird to be seen. They started giggling, saying they had no idea where they could be. Then their PJ shirts would move, and their bellies would peep. Apparently they had decided the baby birds were a little chilly and would be much cozier against their warm bellies. Very cute Mom, but also pretty stinky. The room, not the kids. Well, who am I kidding; the kids too.

We had built the duck coop out of your parent's old kitchen cabinets, using a skid as the base. The turkey coop was Dad's old truck cap we found in the back field. Can you hear the banjo playing? Nothing had to be fancy, it would all be covered in poop soon enough. Finally the day came and all the birds moved outside. Phew.

One day late that summer the kids and I decided to make a fort out of hay bales in the hayloft of the old horse barn – now what we call the pig barn. We had a blast. The next day I went up to get some hay, and ...found a chicken. Weird. When the kids got home from school I asked them about it. One of the boys piped up.

"Well Mom, we had so much fun yesterday building forts that I thought Brownie would like it too. So this morning I brought him up the ladder so he could hang out in the fort for the day." His eyes were so big and brown and full of sweetness Mom, it totally melted my heart. That's why kids are so cute, and also it totally saves their butt sometimes. I know you know what I mean; I was downright adorable.

That summer we also got an above ground pool. The kids absolutely loved it, even though good ol' helicopter Mom made them wear their life jackets that first year. They couldn't yet touch the bottom, and seeing as how we only had a step ladder to get in it at that time, I just didn't trust myself to get in there fast enough if I had to.

Don't get me wrong though Mom, as country as our kids are – they LOVE screen time. When they were babies I thought I'd never plunk them in front of the boob tube. Wrong. I have realized now that T.V. is the best free babysitter out there. There have been many, many days where Chris and I HAD to get stuff done, and we'd plant them in front of the T.V. At least if they were watching TV I knew they weren't killing each other or sticking a knife in the toaster. Sometimes you just gotta do what you gotta do.

Finally the day came that summer to send the meat birds to "The Spa". I was so glad, they really stunk. I borrowed some crates, filled them with chickens and carefully put them on a big tarp in the van. The boys came along for the ride. After buckling them in, they sweetly asked why the chickens didn't wear seatbelts too. I carefully explained they don't make chicken seatbelts and Mommy would drive extra carefully. They spent the whole hour and fifteen minute drive there telling them how fun they were to play with, and how tasty they were going to be. They "got it".

We finally got to the abattoir. Once I parked, a lady who was waiting her turn came up to my window to say hello. I blindly reached down while talking to grab one of our fridge magnets for her. My hand went into something wet, warm and squishy. I just assumed I had stuck my finger in the empty yoghurt container from the morning drive. I looked down. My jaw dropped. She stopped midsentence when she saw the look on my face. What happened was a true testament to farm life.

A chicken had somehow projectile pooped through the side of the crate and it had splattered up between the front seats and all over my phone and wallet. That is what I had put my hand into. BARF!

We unloaded the birds and then drove home, to turn around three hours later and do the drive again to pick them up. The entire chicken run took us about 5 hours. It is safe to say we sang Ol'Anderson's had a farm at least 150 times. Yah, THAT never got old.

I brought the chickens home and stuffed them all tightly into a freezer. When the first customer came three days later to pick up their birds, I realized only the top layer was frozen. I hadn't left enough space in between them for the cold air to circulate. So in actual fact, I was selling three day old chickens. Tom was thrilled.

I had to be proactive to shut him up. I started studying all kinds of bacteria, their lifespan, when they grow best, and what kills them. Food safety isn't something to mess with. After everything I read I wasn't comfortable selling them, so I didn't. I had to listen to my gut. Needless to say Mom we ate a ton of chicken that year, we all lived and I could sleep at night.

To get ready for the pigs we built a big paddock off the old horse barn and cut a hole in the side of it so they could come and go as they pleased. We built a proper lean-to off the barn to give them shade too. The kids were helping us that day, and made a slide out of the 12' boards waiting to be put up and were having a ball. Thank goodness for thick jeans, pulling slivers out of their butts was definitely NOT on the whiteboard. I love their imagination, but wow Mom; sometimes I never know what they'll get up to next.

We were finally set up and the pigs came. Baby pigs are so darn cute! A couple of months later I sent the kids out one morning to feed them. If they want bacon, they have to help out too right? Shortly after my Mom 'Spidey' sense told me to check on them. I started walking towards the barn and heard the kids giggling as they waved at me.

They had apparently grown 2 feet taller in the last 5 minutes. Turns out they were pig surfing – each had one foot on a pig as they were all lined up side by side at the feeder. Little devils.

Those first six months were definitely a lesson in learning from your mistakes. I had pretty much screwed up any income we were supposed to make from veggies and chickens, but would know better for next year. I wasn't discouraged at all though Mom. I knew there would be mistakes, but I also knew, as you always taught me, that is how you learn. If you are afraid to fail, you will never fly. And oh Mom, did we ever have wings!

I'm not looking for a hero biscuit here either Mom, but remember I did all this running around, planting and building with a separated shoulder. And let me tell you, it hurts even more the second time. It made no difference though, I was so determined; nothing could have slowed me down.

The best part about everything Mom was how happy, truly happy I was. Above all we had done what we set out to do that first spring. People were interested in our Farm and we now had livestock. The feeling of accomplishment was incredible. We had so much momentum, we felt unstoppable.

Chapter 3

"No one can make you feel inferior without your consent."

- Eleanor Roosevelt

Bringing Them Home

The fall seemed to show up in the blink of an eye that first year. With it came Blue, an 8 week old Australian Sheppard puppy we'd agreed to babysit for the weekend. He was a black and grey fluff ball with paws bigger than his head, who lived for head pats and belly rubs. I went out one day to find the kids locked together at the shoulders, they had built him a human tent to give him shade. So cute! Stella was having an absolute ball playing with him too. I knew by lunch that first day he wasn't going home.

We now had three chest freezers set up in the 'meat shop', which is what we had turned the lean–to beside the garage into. Beside the freezers was a 4'x 8'chalkboard with our prices, set up above my wooden university desk hosting a scale, pen and paper. I was a little embarrassed as we weren't properly set up like other farm stores, but then I'd gently remind myself that Rome wasn't built in a day.

Our business was growing as fast as our 'to do' list. We already had a waiting list for our soon to arrive beef, and pork was steadily going out the door from our summer oinkers. It felt great; it was really starting to take shape.

I was very conscious of the language that I used, just like you always taught me. Instead of "we will try to" or "we hope to", I'd say "we will', or "we are going to".

I was telling a friend about this and she said there was a guy on YouTube I should check out. YouTube, Mom, is a website made up only of videos, where you can group them all together and have your own "channel". You can find videos on there about absolutely anything. The guy she had recommended turned out to be a Japanese Doctor who'd done some pretty cool experiments.

Dr. Masaru Emoto's most famous work on language was his rice experiment. He took two salt shakers and filled them each halfway with cooked rice. One was labelled love, the other hate. Over the next few weeks he talked to each shaker using the attached emotion, and the rice began to react. The difference was astounding. The "hate" rice would mold far sooner than the "love" rice. Very neat.

Another small change that made a huge difference was replacing the word "but" with something better. It would change my tone from reactive to proactive.

"We have to dig a 50' trench, *but* we don't have the time." OR...

"We have to dig a 50' trench and *we will have to* prioritize our time to get it done."

"I want to double our sales in the next six months *but* I don't have the inventory."

OR...

"I want to double our sales in the next six months so *we need to figure out* how to ramp up our storage space."

Chris and I were working night and day, side by side and we loved every minute of it. To this day we have never had a fight Mom, 'discussions' for sure, but never a harsh word or a raised voice. We just don't get excited about the small stuff other couples seem to. Life is too damn short.

You know what's so great about us Mom? Of course we love each other, but we honestly really like each other too, even after all these years. He is the first person I want to see in the morning, and the last one I want to kiss before bed. I completely understand that expression now, "my other half".

Our main goals over the next two months were to be ready for the cows coming the end of October and get a website going. Our whiteboard was absolutely jam packed with tasks and deadlines with no wiggle room. The cows were coming, we *had* to be ready. This is when we really learned how to prioritize. It was framed in three columns – today, this week and this month, the system we still use today.

The cows that first year would be sharing the pig barn with the oinkers. It had sunken a lot over the last twenty years. Earlier that summer Chris painstakingly used a hydraulic jack and inch by inch, corner by corner he lifted the barn to its original height. We used cinder blocks to hold it up, and then used some old tin as siding, covering the barn's new legs. Amazing what we could find to use once we started poking around.

The water line Dad had put in years ago running to the pig barn needed replacing. We rented a machine and Chris dug out the trench. Mom, it's so great to be married to a man who literally can do anything, just like Dad. Chris has been operating heavy equipment for 25 years now and is so smooth, his old boss used to say he could pick a pimple off someone's back with a machine. Now that's precision.

It was pretty nostalgic watching the kids run up and down the empty trench. They were covered in mud head to toe with smiles ear to ear, just as Ryan and I were back in the '80's when the first trench went in. Sometimes the apple doesn't fall far from the tree I guess. Speaking of which, the apple tree out front is absolutely massive now. I have a bench under it pointed so we can sit and watch the sunsets. Nature always makes the best T.V.

We got the water line in and installed the automatic heated waterer just behind the barn in the middle of the fence, so cows on both sides would be able to get a drink. That was top of our list – having clean unfrozen water for them year round. If you want to see me completely lose my mind, give me water problems. I know you know what I mean.

I remember every spring growing up our water would go brown for a few days with the runoff from the neighbour's cow field. We'd have to go and fill those big blue camping jugs with water from that natural spring just off Carp Road. What a pain in the butt.

I still remember the day you completely lost it. You came home and the water still wasn't good enough to drink yet. You threw a bowl across the kitchen, hopped in the Chevette and took off. Being a Mom now, trying to run a household with water problems, I totally get it. I'm so glad you guys spent the money and put in a new 35' well, and we never had to deal with poo water again.

The day came to pour the foundation in the barn. The cement truck driver was obviously a Dad, and a damn good one. He handed over the controller to William, who needed both of his chubby little hands to hold it. He listened intently to the man's instructions, careful to keep checking if he was doing it right. He did an amazing job and controlled the flow of cement for the whole barn floor. He was so proud of himself, all because somebody let him try. The barn was now ready for cows, another huge checkmark off the list.

We had bought a bull with the herd but weren't set up with a separate area for him. We found a buyer who'd pick him up from the original farm. I got a call one morning saying the trailer was there for the bull but he wouldn't be loaded until he was paid for. I had meant to drop off the cheque the week before, but it hadn't made it to the whiteboard and had completely slipped my mind. Crap.

I flew there at lightning speed. I was so embarrassed and was apologizing profusely. Then I looked down and realized I hadn't changed, and was doing my first business cattle transaction in fluffy pink bunny pajamas.

Chris and I were working ridiculously long hours at this point coming close to the final crunch. We finished all of the fencing for the paddocks, finally. Last checkmark, phew. We had done it, we were ready. It felt amazing Mom..

The end of October came, and so did our cows. It took a few trips to get everybody home, which thankfully were uneventful. Except for, of course, how right after he loaded the first batch of cows on, a tire on the trailer blew. Thankfully he hadn't left yet, so he unloaded the cows, fixed the tire and loaded them again.

The farmer had weaned the six calves two weeks before, separating them from their pregnant Moms. The calves went in one pen, the Mama's in the other. We now had cows on the Farm. We were officially beef farmers. Ya–freakin–hoo!

The first morning after they came we looked outside and all the cattle were together again, the gate separating them completely crushed. I guess we shouldn't have chinsed out and bought the cheap gates. Lesson learned, move on.

Thankfully Brian (the guy we bought the herd from) gave us some great advice to easily move the herd between pastures. Picture a cow with a bubble 5 feet around it; it's called their "flight zone". The moment you walk into that bubble, even one foot inside, the cow will move exactly

180° in the opposite direction. Such a great trick to use when moving cattle. We separated them again and hung a stronger gate.

While we were preparing for cows, another big project was going on here too. Remember the huge 80' x 100' building that had a small hole in the roof? Well, since you left the hole got a heck of a lot bigger, years of weather and winds now had everything inside in disarray. The building had to come down.

This was a hard one Mom. Taking down and getting rid of something that as a family we spent so much time building together growing up. I know it was really hard for Dad too, but he was so good about it. Of course he had to make the odd comment here and there when we were looking for a piece of wood 'yay' big, or a certain size nut that if the building was still here he could have put his hand on it, right on it. And you know Dad; he would have been able to in a second.

Somehow an older fella in his late 60's from Pakenham heard about the job and offered to take it down for us. We agreed. Over the next three months he showed up every day with a smile and one or two other guys in a pickup truck. They took down that entire building and cleaned up most of the mess. Definitely a memorable lesson about not judging a book by its cover.

He phoned us one morning while he was visiting Fred from across the road, who had an old shed he wanted to get rid of and did we want it? You betcha! The older gentleman slid it on his tilt trailer with a chain, brought it over here and slid it off onto the gravel pad we had prepared. You have to love the barter system, our payment to Fred for his old shed – a case of beer. And again, the banjo played.

Later that fall I got a call from a woman who was writing about local entrepreneurs and would I like to be interviewed? Sure! We were so early on in the business I didn't really know what to talk about Mom, but hey – free exposure, sign me up. She spent an hour here getting the tour, the history and the vision behind our business. I remember how impressed she seemed and I was really flattered. The article was published a week after her visit.

I read it and was completely blown away by what we had accomplished in such a short time – through someone else's eyes. I shared the article on Facebook and lots of people added their heartwarming comments. Sales definitely went up following it too, a lovely bonus.

Fast forward to midwinter. The cows had settled in nicely. We had gotten to know them all, each with their distinctive personalities. Bordering their teenage years, the calves were my favourite, Rocky and Whitey being at the top of the list.

Rocky was a beautiful chocolate colour, much darker that the rest. He was not as shy as the others and would come right up for pats, very laid back and trusting. Whitey was hilarious. He would follow you around the field, not three feet behind you. When you would turn around to face him, he would stop and look up and to the side, thinking somehow that made him invisible. You'd turn and start to walk again, and you could hear him match you step for step. I'd stop and turn around – again the gaze to the sky. Twit.

The roof of pig barn where the cows lived that first winter was too low for the tractor to drive in, so we'd have to clean it weekly by hand with a pitchfork and a wheel barrow and then we'd have to hand bomb in fresh straw.

We went through our small square bales way faster than expected. Cows, as we learned poop A LOT! Fred had kindly given us some straw, big bales – 4' x 3' by 5' long. Only thing was, we didn't have a building to store them in yet so after a few snowfalls and cold nights, they were now frozen solid.

One night there was a blizzard, the wind so strong the snow was blowing horizontally. One of those winds were you have to have you back to it or it will take your breath away. Our teeth were frozen chicklets and our fingers were so cold it hurt to use them, even with two good pairs of mitts on. Gotta love Canadian winters!

We were trying to separate a big bale of frozen straw into its individual flakes. It was like trying to separate chapters in a book that had orange juice spilled on it, all the pages now stuck together. We'd pick up the big bale with the tractor forks, lift it as high as we could and then drop it hoping it would pop apart for us. Not so much. Then we tried using shovels to separate it. It was like trying to break apart frozen hamburger patties stuck together using a toothpick. Good times.

We had to scream to hear each other over the howling wind. We were so frustrated, so, so frustrated and tired and cold but it had to be done, and we got it done. Thank goodness we work so well together, and are great at keeping each other's spirits up.

That is an important lesson we quickly learned that first year of farming. There is no 1–800–dial–a–farmer to call and someone will swoop in and take over. It is all up to you. It doesn't matter if you don't know what to do – you keep trying different things until something works.

I have to admit, there is something I didn't count on with raising animals. I had this idea that when they have everything they need, lots of fresh hay and grass, clean water and secure fencing your job is done. Nope. They're living things, and just like people, things happen to them. Pink eye, abscesses, abrasions, pneumonia, all fun things we've had to deal with. The emergency vet number is now on speed dial. Some months I think we pay his whole mortgage.

Just like you always said Mom, you'll never meet more compassionate or more knowledgeable people than veterinarians. And it's not only about how much they know about animal physiology, but how they know so many great tricks to work with them and keep everybody safe – both people and the animals.

One thing's for sure Mom, you'll never hear me complain about a vet bill. Murphy's Law, when you need them it's always after hours in the worst weather. Regardless, they always show up with their toolkit and a smile and are pleasant their whole visit. They never make you feel guilty for having dragged them out of bed in the early morning. There is no way we could be where we are without the awesome team of vets helping us. Very, very grateful.

We had a blast that winter with the kids. At the time we had two snowmobiles – old and tired but we didn't care, we were so lucky they were still running, again all because of Chris' many talents. We'd hook up a long rope to the back of one and then tie it to a sled and take the kids ripping through the fields. So much fun. As long as they had warm dry clothes and a full belly, they were happy to do it for hours. I have so, so many great memories of doing the same thing growing up here on the Farm. Such a great way to get outside and enjoy winter.

That winter when I wasn't playing with the munchkins, feeding cows or shovelling poop my butt was glued in front of my computer. I was building our website, carefully crafting our message and what we were offering. I had no idea then about setting up a PayPal account, pixels, algorithms or marketing strategies. I turned into a Nerdy McNerdster watching YouTube videos, reading articles and taking as many free on-line courses as I could. It's not how bad you want something; it is how hard you are willing to work for it. You were always such a great example of that.

Working so many hours on the computer, my brain often turned to mush. I had to find a way to be more efficient with my time, so I started researching how to be more productive. I began using the Pomodoro method, where you work in segments, with breaks in between.

I'd set up a timer and work for 20 minutes, then take a break for 5 minutes and *allow* myself to do something that required absolutely no brain power. Usually I would dance around like a fool. I love dancing as much as ever Mom, still rockin' the 'Saturday Night Fever' disco moves – they never get old. Then after my timed break – right back at it.

That is something that I still always make time for – going out dancing. My favourite thing to do, but really I only do it once or twice a year. Usually when I hear a good band is playing, I call up Jessica and head over there for the night. Her hubby, she and I enjoy a nice dinner out and then head to a live show. I still dance with my eyes closed Mom with my hair flailing about. So thankful for those nights, it is always so great to catch up with her.

And speaking of close friends, Sammy and Dana are still at the top of my list. It's been 20 years now we have been best friends and let me tell you Mom, they have been behind me through it all. They helped me so much through losing you, starting a business, dealing with anxiety and just getting through the madness of life in general. They are doing amazingly, of course, such incredibly strong independent women. I am so grateful for having them in my life, other than our family and Dad, they are my rocks.

The emails were now pouring in by late fall. I would reply with novels about our farming practices, going on and on about every little detail. I look back and realize how far we have come. Back then I would be crushed if an inquiry didn't lead to a sale. Now I answer with short, concise answers directing them to our website. If they don't buy something – Oh well, at least they have heard about us, maybe they'll even tell a friend.

By this time we had some beef in the freezer for sale, keeping the same pricing as the farmer we bought the herd from. Sales had been steadily increasing, but with the cold weather they had really slowed down, even though we were still delivering right to people's front door. Weird.

Many of those cold winter nights I'd spend in the barn sitting with the animals, often with Rocky's head nudging me for more pats. It would take my mind off the mile long to – do list and my stress would fall away. No matter how crappy or hard the day had been, sitting with them always relaxed me and reminded me what made it all worthwhile, and why we were doing what we were doing.

Chris was snowplowing for the City which had him gone most of the time, working days 7 – 7, weekends included. It was a real adjustment being alone on the Farm all the time that first winter. Farm tours came to a halt when it got really cold. People aren't really into walking around in a foot of snow when it was minus thirty, and I can't blame them. It honestly was fine though Mom, I was happy for the change, and to have more time to myself.

So many nights after the kids were finally asleep I probably should have hit the hay but I would stay up just to have time alone, treasuring the solitude, peace and quiet. No distractions or demands, only me and my peanut butter cups. Perfect.

I'd watch YouTube videos about surprise marriage proposals, amazing X factor auditions, a deaf person hearing for the first time, stuff like that. No matter what mood I was in, they would always make me smile. There is nothing like watching someone experience pure joy, I just love it. I would read about 'famous' people too, who worked their ass off to get that way.

J.K. Rowling, who wrote Harry Potter, was too poor for photocopying so she'd manually type out each manuscript by hand to send to prospective publishers. The first few rejected her, and then one didn't. You wouldn't believe how big Harry Potter became after you left Mom. It's not just one movie anymore. There's a series of films, of books and a whole world of merchandise – all because she refused to give up. She said one of my favourite quotes – "Rock bottom became the solid foundation on which I rebuilt my life."

One writer was so broke before he got famous that he and his wife had to borrow clothes for their wedding, and get rid of their phone line because they couldn't afford it. His first short story was rejected 60 times before it got published. He ended up doing alright though. His name is Steven King.

I was working really hard on the Farm, and really, really enjoyed the social media aspect of the business. It had proven to be the absolute best way to get the word out about us. Again Mom, I can't even describe how much a part it is in people's everyday lives.

One thing though with the popularity of social media now, it's so easy to get caught up in comparing yourself to others. Worrying about what you 'should be' doing or what your life is 'supposed to' look like. I would follow other Farms and get a little jealous at how easy it all seemed for them, from what they were posting. Yes, there were so many moments that were so beautiful they would take my breath away, but also some days were not as fun as others. It was all part of the deal.

I was posting about all the bad *and* the good, and made sure to always point out the rainbow. More than anything I wanted to inspire people to keep following their dreams, even when, especially when, everything goes wrong, and use us as an example of what you can achieve when you do.

We finished that winter with a website up and running and happy cows that had made themselves at home. It was a real wake up call to go through that first winter with cattle, never ending computer work, two crazy kids and missing Chris like crazy. It was a great lesson in perseverance and keeping our eye on the big picture. We had already gotten so much done, and we had so much great energy keeping us going. We had some pretty big plans for the upcoming season and we couldn't wait for the snow to melt and to get back to working side by side, building and growing. It's what we do best.

Chapter 4

"You learn more from losing than winning.

Your learn how to keep going."

-   Morgan Wootten

Just Keep Going

I'll be honest Mom, snow blowing the quarter mile long driveway, keeping the woodstove going 24/7 and winter chores in my Gumby snowsuit were all wearing pretty thin by the spring of 2013. We were thrilled to soon be working without icicles hanging from our noses, and only be wearing one layer of clothing.

Our vision remained the same – sell meats but we'd skip a year on the veggies. Our goals for that spring and summer were to build a bigger garden, drill a new well, get through calving, get our hay off and into storage, and build a big barn for the cows. No sweat.

It was clear from the year before that I had absolutely no idea what I was doing with commercial gardening. I had bought a computer program the past winter for CSA planning, all based on formulas. It did all the figuring out for me. That spring I'd plant as if I were doing a CSA, and learn exactly how much time was needed for seeding, weeding and watering. Whatever didn't go to farm visitors would go to the pigs. Nothing would be wasted.

One thing was for sure, we needed a much, much bigger garden. We decided to take a large area beside the side lawn and turn that into a 50' x 100' garden.

Chris tilled up the area for me and we ordered some soil, a bunch of soil – 45 tonnes to be exact. After spreading it as best I could with the tractor, I raked the whole garden into beds – by hand! My arms grew about 2 inches in the process and my shoulder hated me but it had to be done. I loved that there was absolutely no pressure with the garden this year. If I screwed up again, it didn't matter, at least I was learning. It's all about perspective right?

I wanted to get more involved with the local food movement too, and learn as much as I could. I started sitting in on meetings and going to local conferences or anywhere I could to connect more with people in the industry. The most wonderful thing about farming and farmers I soon learned is that it's completely different than any other industry. It's all about collaboration and co–operation, and not about competition. Every person I met was happy to take time with me and share what they'd learned about growing food and a food business. They were all so great to be around, and had so much to offer. Being with them I knew would just fire up my passion even more.

At one meeting I met Katie, a veggie CSA grower who lives 10 minutes away. We hit it off right away and she came over a few days later. We decided to do a veggie CSA program together the following summer.

She'd start all of the seedlings at her place, bring them here and I'd plant them, grow them and harvest them. She'd pick up the veggies twice a week and deliver them. She was too busy lambing during the spring to garden, and I didn't want to have to leave the farm to deliver. It was a perfect arrangement. It's so true Mom, a simple hello really can lead to a million things.

That spring Lake Louise appeared again out in the front field. It's so neat Mom, because it doesn't look at all like there is a huge dip in the field until all the snow melts, and we are left with our own private little lake.

The kids went out one morning in Chris' rubber boots. So cute watching from the kitchen window as they tried to walk their tiny little legs in boots that came up to their mid thighs. They waded slowly out into the lake, and of course had to push the limits. They were seeing just how close they could get to having the water level come almost up to the top of their boots, but not over.

And of course, they both took one step too far. I could see from the house the look of shock on their faces when the icy cold water filled their boots. They sloshed their way back to the house with their teeth chattering and their legs surely popsicles. I had towels, dry socks and cozy pants ready for them. The kettle was on for hot chocolate, just like you did when Ryan and I did the exact same thing years ago.

Speaking of water, no way was I going to run the risk of running out of water again this year. We had to secure a permanent, reliable water source on the Farm. Sound familiar??? Dad knew that there was an old well in the back yard, somewhere, that had been covered over years before. We just had to find it. Luckily he remembered where the fellow lived who your Dad bought the farm from. I stopped by and he had an old photo of the back yard with the well in it. At least we had an idea of where to start looking.

We rented an excavator and Chris started digging, again blowing me away with his skills. We eventually found it only to discover it had collapsed and was useless. Crap. Huge hole in the backyard, mud everywhere, the excavator bill to be paid and still no water. We'd have to bite the bullet and drill a new well. At least we tried right?

We hired a local company, the same one that did yours actually, and they began digging. When he did find water, he found lots of it. We would never run out of water again. I was thrilled. I had it tested for E. coli and coliform and both were negative. Phew. It shut Tom up; as he had been hinting maybe the water was contaminated. Now we just had to live through another season of mud and mess in both the side and backyard. At least it gave the kids hours of fun.

They'd be so covered in mud and muck Mom; their clothes were caked with it. I wouldn't even let them near the house until I hosed them off – the kids I mean, forget the clothes. Good thing I was getting them from Sally Ann, they were growing so fast often their pants would be so far gone with holes and rips after only a few weeks of being worn I'd just toss them.

I honestly don't understand people who spend $50 on a pair of pants that will only fit their kids for a few months, and then helicopter like mad over them to stay clean. To me, there is absolutely nothing better than letting your kids just be kids. That's a happy childhood. That was my childhood.

And speaking of the kids, they were getting more and more inventive with their shenanigans, now being the ripe old ages of 5 and 6. I was giving a farm tour that spring to a couple and their three little kids when a friend showed up – remember Wendy Mom? The girl I did my first backpacking trip across Europe with? She drove in at just the right time that day.

I had just showed the family the pigs, and we were on our way to see the chickens, ducks and turkeys. I saw Wendy come around the garage, she waved hello and at the same time we both heard a lot of giggling and then "Hey Mom!" It was our kids. It was our kids standing on the ROOF of the garage! Wendy saw them, looked at me and shot me an "I got this" look. She's a Mom of four now and can handle anything. I continued my tour without missing a beat, the family none the wiser.

After they left I called for the kids. They bounced across the yard towards me, "What Mom?" As if they didn't know. Little devils.

Turns out they had taken a bunch of our stacking vegetable crates, used them to make steps and get them onto the roof of the meat shop, then up onto the garage roof. "Aren't you happy Mom, we put our heads together and figured it out." Again, one of those moments as a parent you're secretly proud but have to act perturbed.

So back to the well...

Someone had mentioned to me it might be a good idea to get a heavy metals test on the new well. It was 300 bucks but if there was anything funky I wanted to know before we used it. This of course woke Tom up again. He waited patiently, as did I for the results...

We got the test back and it turns out there was above average numbers in four areas. The whole time Tom was laughing and chanting – "I told you so". Forget him I thought. I'll just do a ton of research and learn how to fix it – no problem.

I read a bunch of articles and talked to different government departments. Three of the four high levels would be fine, but the forth one was a big problem. The water had far too much salt in it – 500 ppm (parts per million) to be exact. The maximum level veggies could stand was 150 ppm. At least we could use it for the animals...

I researched a little more and found out that high salt water content could potentially kill the pigs. They sweat out of their hooves so too much salt in their water could clog the pores and they could overheat and die. The salt could give the birds heart attacks. It would make the cows thirstier, never feeling as if they had enough, and they would just keep drinking more, never quenching their thirst. Arg!

Tom just loved this and his chanting was getting louder. What a jerk. I was determined to find a solution. Everybody in the world seems to have a water system to purify their water, so why couldn't we? An expensive solution I assumed, but whatever. We had just spent $12,000 on the new well – what's a little more?

We brought out some water specialists from two different water companies. They said they could try and install a system that would remove the salt. It would be $5,000 – $7000 but they couldn't guarantee it would get the salt out. They were quite honest and said they had never seen levels so high, and were very doubtful that it would work at all.

ARG! We were screwed, and there was nothing we could do about it. But you know what Mom? At least we learned all of this before we used it and lost anybody, so I was very grateful for that. And really, in the grand scheme of things, which is what I always remind myself of when a problem seems too big, the truth is that we were still all happy and healthy – bottom line. Billions of people around the world are starving to death; meanwhile our biggest hurdle was that we had lost a little money.

And really, at least the kids had another summer of mud city to keep them happy right? Again, I can't thank you enough Mom for teaching me to always see through rose coloured glasses. I have a saying now, "If your glass seems half empty – pour it in a smaller glass." I actually coined a phrase Mom, I don't share it with too many people for obvious reasons, "If you don't have a pot to piss in, well at least you don't have to wash the pot!" It's all about perspective.

We had six pregnant cows that would calve that spring. Very exciting and also totally nerve racking. What if I had to stick my hand up a cow's woo woo?

One morning one of the cows was lying off by herself in the field with something coming out of her back end. Holy cow it was happening! I called Brian, the farmer we had bought the herd from and he flew to our house, as he said he'd help us with our first calving. We walked down the field together. I was vibrating with excitement, which quickly turned to dismay as he said with a low voice, "That doesn't look good at all".

It turns out she was not calving at all – she had a prolapsed rectum. She had slipped on the mud in the night, and fell with her back legs not underneath her but behind her. The strain of her constant attempts had her rectum prolapse. Her eyes were full of panic and she was exhausted. Poor girl.

I fetched a bucket of warm water and a small towel. Brian gently washed off what was coming out and pushed it back in. We propped a bail of straw under her side so she'd be more upright, giving her more of a chance to find her feet.

We had to rotate her body – basically keep flipping her from one side to another every few hours with ropes so her main nerves wouldn't be pinched and leave her paralyzed. Let me tell you Mom, it's no easy feat flipping a cow. Those suckers are heavy.

We did this the rest of the day and throughout the night, as well as make sure she always had hay and a fresh bucket of water right near her head. If she didn't get up within 24 hours, chances are she wouldn't get up again.

The next day was Mother's Day. It had now been about 30 hours since we first found her. Charles came happily bouncing down the field, muddy rubber boots, wearing one of his Chris' tattered farm coats hanging past his knees screaming "Happy Mother's Day!" He asked me what I was doing. "Oh honey, her bum fell out, so I'm helping put it back in." Somehow it made perfect sense to him.

"Well, we made you pancakes! When you're done with the bum come and get'm!" I finished washing her rectum and put it back in her yet again, but it was pointless. I came in, ate the pancakes, praised the boys for their tastiness, and then quietly made the call. We had to do what was right, she was suffering.

A man with a truck showed up shortly after, he took out his gun and I led him to the cow. He reassured me that we had done everything we could and this was the very last resort.

Other than that I had an amazing Mother's Day. The kids completely spoiled me with homemade cards, foot massages, tickle fights and warm cuddles. They totally brightened my day. Amazing how little people can make such a big difference.

We could have boo–hooed all day and had the world's biggest pity party, but this was simply a fluke of nature. We weren't the worst farmers in the world. This was just one really crappy thing that happened and it wasn't our fault. I remembered one of Dad's best sayings – hard times make good people.

We had done the best we could, and that was all we could do. I was really proud of us. I knew that day that we could handle anything that came our way, as long as we always looked at the bright side. And of course I would always lighten the mood telling one of my famous terrible one liner jokes. You know how much I have always loved them.

I've heard a ton related to farming and food in the last little while so don't be surprised if they show up here and there throughout the letter, just for fun. Here's one of my favourites, but way too inappropriate to share with customers or a Facebook page, but I know you'll appreciate the humour;

What do you call a cow masturbating in a field?

Beef stroganoff! HA HA!

The next few calves came without incident – thankfully. The first two we named Miss April and Chance. Miss April made her appearance a week after Mother's Day. I noticed something out of the back end of a cow, and ran down the field. I could see it was the head and front hooves of a calf dangling out. Wahoo!

All of a sudden, she got up and started walking to the hay feeder. Hell of a time to be having a snack eh?! Can't blame her though, I totally understood. I ordered a donair to the delivery room with one of the boys. I was getting pretty hangry and was determined to chow down between contractions. The nurses were pretty annoyed, telling me I would just end up throwing it up. "Oh well, better get a bedpan ready then." They didn't see the humour in it, but personally, I thought I was hilarious.

The emerging calf was now halfway out and swinging back and forth as she walked. Her body gave one big push and down dropped the baby – right on its head! She instinctively turned around and started cleaning it up. By this time Chris had made it back from getting the kids on the bus. We stood silently and watched in amazement.

The next 10 minutes were absolutely magical Mom. Little Miss April found her legs, as wobbly as they were and got up to a standing position. She practiced her first few steps, the odd time falling but always getting back up. She waddled over and started smashing her head up and down under her Mama's neck. That's what calves do to get milk down in the udder. After a few more bumps she got the stronger scent from a few feet back, stumbled towards it, found the jackpot and immediately started nursing. It was incredible.

Little did we know how much time we would spend over the next few years watching and waiting for that special moment. Some farmers supplement and bottle feed their calves, but we always wanted to do everything as naturally as possible. Besides, I had been milked by our babies for a total of four years and I was absolutely done with night – time feedings if I could help it.

The next calf came a few days after Miss April, and we named him Chance. His birth was smooth and unassisted, the challenge came after. After three hours of watching him walk around and not going for a drink we knew that we had to do something.

We had to get them both into a smaller area, and then get the Mama into a 'chute', to milk her into a bottle then force – feed it to the calf. A chute is like a very tiny hallway no longer or wider than a cow. The cow walks into it, thinking they'll walk right through but then doors close on its neck keeping it in place, so you can work with it safely.

We bought a chute with the herd, but of course it wasn't properly set up yet. We got the tractor and brought over the chute and some gates and made a makeshift pen. Somehow we managed to get the Mama into the chute but she wasn't too happy about it. Neither Chris nor I had ever milked a cow before but that day come hell or high water we were going to learn how.

Our chute wasn't a fancy one; you can only access the animal from behind. I was on poop detail, so I'd hold the Mama's tail out of the way, carefully watching her giant raspberry so I could warn Chris before he got splattered. He started milking her – and nothing was coming out. Apparently there was a technique; we just hadn't yet figured it. He kept trying.

At this point a friend of ours had dropped by unexpectedly and walked down the field to find us. She is one of those amazing women who always looks beautiful, her hair done and make–up on. I remember seeing her white sandals and pretty coloured toenails, appreciating all the cow patties she must have dodged on her trek down to us.

She knew by the sweat on our brows and the frustration in our voices that things weren't going well. She offered to help and I politely declined, I just couldn't see it Mom.

The newborn calf at this point was freaking out. I brought him around to the front of the chute and tied him there, so Mama and baby could see each other. During this fiasco, Mom, I turn around and low and behold our friend had hopped the fence, and was milking Mama like a pro, the bottle already half full. Another memorable lesson to not judge a book by its cover. And she was doing it without anyone on poop patrol. Brave soul.

She taught us her trick, and Chris took over. When we had a full bottle Chris held the calf, which isn't easy, calves are small but still very strong and wiggly. I had to keep his mouth open with one hand and squirted the 'white gold' down his throat with the other. He got a big drink and we knew he would be okay. We felt like superstars, it was amazing.

We went through this whole process maybe three more times that day. Fred had once told us this great trick – put food colouring on the cow's teats and then we'd know by looking at the calf's mouth if he had drunk. Thankfully by the end of the day we could see he had, hence the name Chance. Had he not figured it out, there was a good 'chance' we would be stuck with a bottle fed calf. Sounds cute and all, however, I knew the novelty of more work would soon wear off. We had enough to do. And speaking of white gold…

How do you keep your milk from going sour?

Keep it in the cow! HA HA!

Fred was born a week after Chance and picked up nursing right away – thankfully. He was my favourite of the whole herd. He had huge, soft brown eyes, and wasn't nearly as skittish as the other calves. He and Whitey were my buddies, Fred loving the head scratches, Whitey still the "invisible" stalker.

Now that calving was over we had to figure out what to do for breeding. The options were to get a bull or use artificial insemination. The latter option means you have to watch for who is in heat: you know because they'll keep trying to hump someone. Then you have a 12–18 hour window to get some papa juice in them. Seeing as how we had better things to do than watch for potential cow porn all day, we decided to get a bull.

A few weeks later we found our Prince. He was a Hereford purebred Canadian Champion, and very much a gentle giant. He would quietly walk around with his confident slow swagger, his big bull dingle berries swaying to and fro, eyeing up his next date. I soon learned there's no flirting, no "Hey, can I buy you a drink?" in the cow world. He would just saunter right up to a lady, stick his nose right in her woo–woo, decide if it was to his liking and then Shebang! Off he went.

Within a couple of months of his arrival he wasn't mounting anyone anymore. All of our cows were now bred for the following season.

As well as everything that was going on, Chris built the most beautiful deck for the pool. It's the entire length of the house, and wraps almost a quarter of the way around the pool on both sides. We now have a picnic table on it, and there's still lots of room for lawn chairs and drying racks for laundry. .Again, amazing to watch him build, and how quickly and efficiently he works. Such a stud muffin.

And I have to mention too Mom, how helpful Dad has been with all of our building and different projects over the years. It has been an absolute pleasure to watch him and Chris work together on so many different things, both at our house and his. It's neat to watch because they can see problems from different angles, and are great at working together to come up with the best solution.

More than once I definitely felt like I was standing right in your shoes again– cooking them grilled cheese sandwiches for lunch and then hollering out the back door to come in. It's been really good for me to have him around so much. We have become really close over the last few years; I have gotten to know him as a person, not just as a parent.

At his place Mom he built the most amazing shop, his dream shop. It took a few years, and lots of changes to his design but wow Mom, it is so nice to see him finally get something I know he wanted for so long. He even fixed up his parents' old pool table and set up a room for it in the basement. The boys, Chris and I love to go over and sit with Dad, listen to Dire Straits and shoot a few games.

Can't tell you how proud I am when I look at all those plaques of excellence and recognition covering the basement wall that you received, both before and after. You sure were one heck of an accomplished lady

Mom, all because you would never give up on anything you believed in. So inspiring.

We were now growing our own hay for winter feeding, as well as producing our own straw for bedding, bailing what was left after the grains had been harvested. We were officially now a sustainable closed loop farm. We still needed to build a housing facility for all of it though. We refused to go through another winter fighting with frozen bales.

We talked to different farmers and did some shopping around and decided to go with building a coverall. It would go to the left of the big metal bin that still stands, on the Kinburn side, with the farm lane running between both. We found a local company and they soon began. What was SO awesome about it was that it was a young woman doing most of the construction. I loved that. When completed we filled it with all of our hay and straw.

We had spent the past winter figuring out exactly what kind of barn we wanted to build to house the cattle. The pig barn was a great temporary solution, but no way was I spending another winter shovelling poop by hand. We would build it on the same side as the coverall, and build a fence around both for their winter yard. We ended up, after many different versions, going with a 32' x 70' barn, with two huge openings out the back that the tractor could easily fit through.

We ordered the lumber from Harry Barr in Pakenham, who has just this year retired Mom. Pretty neat that this farm has been getting wood from his mill for over 40 years. We found an architect and had the drawings made up and got all necessary permits. It was amazing to finally be breaking ground after so much prep work.

It was incredible to watch Chris build it. He did all of the work himself, with a friend helping out for only a couple of weeks. He was so in his element Mom. It was great to see him doing something he loves so much, and is so bloody talented at. He was going through some pretty big health issues at the same time too, but he never complained once.

It was funny because when the crane operator showed up to help lift the trusses for the roof on, he said he had been here before years ago. There was some young girl living here that tutored him with the theory part when he was going for his driver's licence. It was me! Small world eh?

I remember one afternoon a storm was rolling in, the sky quickly turning from a bright blue to a dismal gray. The wind so strong the trees on the fence line were almost bent over. Chris didn't bat an eyelash and kept on working to secure the beams, finishing what he had to get done.

I know some ladies love a man in a suit, slicked back hair and fancy pointed shoes, but that day looking at him up on that ladder, both shoulders of his T–shirt now stained with brown sawdust and sweat from wiping his forehead, Carhartt pants gently hugging his great butt and his tool belt hanging on his hip, that totally did it for me. He's every bit as hot as when we first got hitched. Nummy.

I have to say too Mom, I love that he still watches me change. Even after all these years and the "shifts" my body has had, (mostly downward) he still makes me feel sexy as hell. And who would have thought your orgasms get even better in your 40's?? You're my Mom, so I won't say too much more on the subject but let me tell you, our marriage just keeps getting better and better – in every way. I am one very happy Scorpio. It's a wonder we don't have 25 kids.

Speaking of which Mom, I have to say thank you. Thank you so much for taking care of me our last day before you left. I had just come from the hospital and found out that our baby had died. You tucked me in on the couch with a cozy blanket and then made me a grilled cheese and a cup of tea.

I remember you laughing at the state of us, you with your hairless head and your breathing tube attached to your oxygen tank, me with, well all that stuff that was happening because of the miscarriage. We shared such a great laugh, member? Makes my heart warm whenever I think of it.

That was a really hard time for me, losing a child and a parent within days. But you know what Mom? I truly believe that Nature always knows what's best, even if we don't understand it. There is no way I would have had a healthy pregnancy if it had continued, not with all the stuff I went through that first year after losing you. It was such a blessing, I whole heartedly believe that. And now she is with you, (I always felt she was a girl) which makes me feel so good. There is absolutely no one I would rather her be with. It gives me so much peace I can't even begin to tell you. Thank you again for being an amazing Mom when I needed you most. You always put me first, right until the last minute. I was so lucky to have you as long as I did.

I am so grateful I could spend every day with you from your diagnosis until the minute you left. How lucky was I to be able to do that??? I am so thankful for those 14 weeks Mom. Not for one minute did I ever complain that I didn't have more time, so many people have none at all. I am grateful for every second. We definitely made the best of it eh? I remember absolutely stuffing our faces with chocolate cake in the hospital cafeteria that day, it didn't stand a chance.

I do have one regret though, the only regret I have in life. I never let you see me cry after you told me you were leaving. I was so damn determined to be strong for you, as I know you were for me – you never shed one tear with me either. Two crazy, strong, passionate and determined women, that's us. I am so, so, so proud to be your daughter, and so friggin' proud to have had you as a Mom.

Back to our farming fiascos...

Our tagline from the start had been "Where does your food come from?" to get people thinking. We had marketed our farm tours to teach kids and it was working. We were now giving tours to girl – guides, home day care groups and lots of families with little people. Not every visit ended in a sale, but at least more people were coming to the Farm and we were getting our name out there. Perfect, except for one thing. Tom would be on those tours too.

At Guelph I had done a project on food safety, and learned about one case where a Mom had used fresh manure in her veggie garden. Something didn't get washed properly and her 8 year old boy died. Remembering that, I became very anxious with so many kids running around the farm, their grubby little hands touching everything. Even with all I had learned about the power of thought, I still somehow had let the poison of anxiety creep in.

What if I hadn't disinfected the plastic picnic table properly and one of the Girl Guides that just ate their lunch on it got sick?

What if someone from the Nursery School visit yesterday somehow got chicken poo on their hands, didn't wash them properly, ate their lunch and then got sick?

I'm sure these questions sound far – fetched Mom but these are actual examples that haunted me. I'd be anxious for days after a children's tour. It was completely irrational and ridiculous. I had to change something, so I backed off on promoting tours for kids, and focused more on marketing to adults.

Outside of farm visitors Tom was generally quiet as long as I went through my by now OCD ritual of washing my hands once and then sanitizing them twice before handling anything. The only potential for catastrophe or death (remember he was the king of Worst Case Scenario possibilities) was if the freezers were to break and the meat to spoil. So I created a daily temperature check list. Simple.

Whenever I had anxiety I worked to figure out the root of it, and then create a system so there wasn't any need to be anxious. It felt so much better to be proactive rather than reactive, it gave me a choice. You always taught me that: you don't like something – change it.

During that summer we had put a fourth side on the Meat Shop. Now it was all closed in and protected from the elements. We now had 6 freezers in total, a commercial fridge, a fancy hanging scale and a cash register. It was now a proper store. It felt amazing, and so much more professional.

We were in great shape going into the fall and winter meat wise. The freezers were full of great product to sell and the coverall was full of beautiful dry hay and straw for the winter.

I was pretty darn busy come the end of that summer in 2013. I was saying yes to everything. I was giving free talks, giving large and small farm tours weekly and delivering meats right to people's front doors. I was exhausted but not at all tired, if that makes any sense. We were just so thrilled with all we had gotten done that year; we were floating on cloud nine. Nothing better than that feeling of accomplishment. It's like a drug, and we were definitely hooked.

Chapter 5

"Change your thoughts and you change your world."

- Norman Vincent Paele

Peeling Back the Onion

We were really looking forward to the change in seasons when the fall came. We had been were working 16 hour days, 7 days a week and needed a break from all the work that came with warmer weather. It didn't seem like work though really, we got to be together and build cool stuff. It was like having a date night every night, we just happened to be in poo covered rubber boots.

I think the key to us having such a great marriage Mom is that we whole heartedly support each other in everything we do. We genuinely want each other to be happy. When we met it was pretty clear that we were both really strong people, full of adventure and ideas – sound familiar?

We both stayed who we were when we started dating, kept up with our friends and our own lives, and have every day since.

Again, you and Dad were such great role models, thank you. You always spoke to each other with respect, and would listen to what the other had to say. It's that simple. If you want to be heard, you have to be ready to listen too. I can honestly say, and I know lots of people I'm sure wouldn't believe me, but being married to him has been the easiest thing I've ever done. Thank you for raising me to see how easy love can be. Cheesy but true.

I was still delivering to Ottawa, but I knew from last winter the farm gate visitors would soon slow down, which was fine. It's hard running a business from your home that is also open to the public. You always have to be ready to smile and offer your time, even when customers show up outside our working hours, and believe me, they did.

One Sunday morning that fall Chris had taken the kids out to give me a break – bless his heart. I was having a lovely long, hot, uninterrupted shower. It was heaven. Then Stella started barking, and kept barking. The more she barked, the more I screamed at her. She wouldn't stop and I lost it, my one moment of peace disrupted. I was now hoarse from yelling, so I hopped out of the shower, threw on a towel and stormed downstairs, cursing like a trucker the whole way.

I turned the corner at the bottom of the red stairs to find customers - a couple and their young daughter - STANDING IN OUR KITCHEN! I was completely speechless. Granted I knew the Mom from college and the Dad from high school from many years before, but still – not cool. I asked them nicely to wait in the store while I got dressed. I made no apologies for my appearance, but did for my potty mouth for their daughter's sake.

With the fall came the joy of loading another batch of pigs onto the trailer. The first batch that year went on with only a little hassle, that fall batch flat out refused. We tried everything – apples, watermelon, all their favourites and nothing worked. Of all the animals we raise – pigs can definitely be the biggest assholes when they want to be. You just can't make a pig do anything it doesn't want to do.

It was almost noon and we had been at it for an hour. By now Chris and I were sweating, bickering, totally worked up and irritated, as were the pigs. That wound me up even more. We would get them halfway up the ramp onto the trailer, then they'd turn around and run right back into the barn, regardless if we were in their way or not. Not much you can do when 250 pounds that's only two feet high smashes into the back of your legs. You're goin' down and that's all there is to it.

I remembered a farmer once saying if you put a bucket on their head; it will make them walk forward. Worth a try, right? I gave it a shot and two seconds later I had a pig sitting on my foot, now a pancake, with a bucket on its head. Suddenly my foot got warmer. Turns out Mr. Chops had a nervous poo. Eventually we got them loaded, they went to the butcher and I washed my boot. Good times.

Our vision evolved that fall. I realized during the past summer how much I enjoyed teaching people about gardening, so I decided to create some workshops over the winter. I wanted the courses to be well thought out, easy to follow with simple and practical takeaways. A lot of the material I would share was what *not* to do; I was an expert on that. Come the end of winter I had four workshops developed and a revenue stream that wasn't weather dependant.

Speaking of income, the animals were now more or less set up and we were ready to really ramp up our meat sales, I just didn't know how. Sales were good but their timing was too unpredictable, which made a constant rotation of meats through the freezers impossible. Another big problem was that people seemed to order certain cuts far more than others.

It's like we were making boxes of crayons, every cut representing a different colour. Everyone wanted the red and blue ones – bacon and sausages, or steaks and burgers and I'd be stuck with whatever was left. I needed a way to move all the meat through the store so the freezers were empty by the time the next batch of meats would arrive.

I emailed a local business coach – Angie Peladeau - who happened to farm too. I remember on her intake form it asked on a scale of one to ten how willing was I to change. I wrote down "20". I clearly needed help and wasn't shy to admit it.

She had me figure out exactly what it cost us to produce a pound of meat, down to the penny - which isn't used anymore by the way. Another important word came into play with pricing – contingency. We had farmed for more than a year now and had realized just how unpredictable things are when you're working with nature. Both our pork and beef prices went up a little bit, and thankfully our customer base at that time didn't mind.

I decided to create a meat CSA. Everything would be a formula, which I loved. Based on how many annual shares we sold, we'd know how many animals to breed and when to process them. We'd still have beef and pork for farm gate customers – but the bulk would be for our CSA. It was great; most of the meat would be sold before we even raised it.

We are four years into our CSA now Mom, and I have to say it runs smooth like butter. It took a heck of a lot of work and figuring out to get to this stage. When I bring home meats now I weigh out four months of CSA baskets right away, ticking off who gets what in "The Book". I make sure everyone get a nice mix throughout the year. Whatever is left is available for farm gate sales.

I deliver once a month to four locations, stopping only for 15 minutes at each. Labelled bags for both CSA and farm gate customers are put in numbered coolers. I bring a list of who gets what, when and which cooler it's in. I am such a nerd for organizing Mom, I love it.

My marketing 'strategy' before that fall of 2013 was atrocious. I basically just kept throwing up pictures of what we had on our Facebook page in hopes someone would buy something. To improve our marketing, I spent lots of time that winter watching free webinars, taking on-line workshops, reading countless articles, researching what time of day was best to post, which day of the week, which types of graphics were most appealing – anything and everything I could think of.

I used everything I learned and launched our Meat CSA and it sold out in less than two months. Wa-freakin-hoo! We'd finally have predictable year round income from meats come spring. Awesome, but I still needed a way to make money throughout the winter. I posted an add offering to clean houses. A little embarrassing but whatever, we had bills to pay and lots of them.

Lisa and Jaime both emailed me right away. They knew I had been landscaping for the past 20 years and their Dad needed some help with his yard. It was great to be working with flowers and gardens again Mom, something I definitely miss now that everything was about food – feathered, furred or fallowed.

I also met with a woman named Rhonda who had two kids, was pregnant and needed help daily to keep up her house. The hours were flexible, the pay was great and she and I hit it off right away.

In her bedroom she had one of those huge Bristol boards hanging, the kind we used for science fair projects when I was a kid. It was filled with inspirational quotes, positive sayings as well as hand written mantras and point form goals with deadlines. The one that caught my eye said "$600,000 by Sept 1st". It was then February.

Rhonda came in and explained it was her vision board. It was easier for her to visualize herself living the life she wanted when it was right there in front of her. It was as full and busy as our whiteboard, but this was full of things she *wanted* to do, not things she *had* to do.

Interesting...

I started wondering what I would put on mine if I made one. Plane tickets for everybody whenever we wanted were my first thought, but then right away I could hear my little voice telling me how things like that don't happen to people like me. I was just a farm girl shovelling poop and growing carrots. Again I went back to the computer, finding more rags to riches stories to help me keep believing in myself;

Oprah Winfrey was so poor growing up she sometimes had to wear potato bags for clothing.

Jim Carrie dropped out of school at 15 to take a job as a janitor to help feed his family, who at the time were so poor they were living out of a van.

Sylvester Stallone ended up selling his dog for $25 to get some cash so he could turn his electricity back on while he was writing Rocky.

I reminded myself again that nobody sees what goes on behind closed doors. I made my own vision board. I pushed myself to think big. The whole time though I could still hear my little voice but I ignored it and kept going anyway.

Many of the things I put on it weren't 'things' at all, but ideas. "Happy Family", "Beach vacations twice a year" and "Financial freedom" were the first three. As well as of course my black Porsche Carrera, my beautiful new laundry room and our bedroom with a stone floor to ceiling fireplace.

I started to challenge the voice in my head, "Why couldn't that happen to me?" "Why do I think I am not good enough?" I wanted to know exactly where deep down my self-doubt lived. I started peeling myself back like an onion, really looking at all the layers that make me 'me'. It's pretty interesting when you take away all the bullshit that you tell yourself, and see what you are really made of.

One day Rhonda told me about a movie called "The Secret". She said the movie was instrumental in helping her change her thinking, adding that after the first few times she watched it and really "got it", she made her first million. HELLO! I ordered the movie on Amazon that night. Chris and I watched it a couple of times over the next few days, and it changed our thinking from that day forward.

The movie talks about the subconscious mind and how so much information is thrown at us every day we can't possibly consciously process it all. The brain takes it and stores it in our subconscious mind, and then this information, whether we realize it or not, is what we use when we make decisions. It gives us our gut feelings and intuition.

I found it all very interesting, so I started reading more about the subconscious, trying to really understand how it worked. I also learned about neuroplasticity, the muscle building part of the brain. Just like any other muscle, I could build it by working on it. I could strengthen it to program my subconscious. Hmmm.

If I wanted positive thinking and believing in myself no matter what to come automatically, I had to consciously make a choice to keep thinking those types of thoughts. The more times I did, I'd be hard-wiring my subconscious to believe it as well too.

I could consciously choose the overflow of information that would get tucked away. Then when faced with obstacles or problems, my gut would be telling me I could do anything, because that is what I had trained it to do with my constant repetition of positive conscious thoughts. Pretty heavy concepts I know Mom, and confusing to grasp but when I did, everything changed for me.

"Until you make the unconscious conscious, it will control your life and you will call it fate." Carl Yung, another pretty smart dude.

The movie talked a lot about the Law of Attraction too. Basically it says that whatever you are focusing on, you will bring more of into your life.

A perfect example would be when you really stub your toe in the morning. It hurts, you get annoyed, it makes you sour and then the rest of your morning seems to go sideways. You can't shake the bad mood and then more and more things happen to keep you cranky. You get back exactly the energy you are putting out.

I know how I tick Mom, but now I know 'why' I tick the way I do. The more confident I am, the more I push my limits, the more risks I take, the more I succeed. The more I succeed, the more confident I am, the more I push my limits, the more risks I take, the more I succeed, and repeat. Of course I'm human and I have days where I get down on myself, but now I know I just have to change my thinking and snap out of it. And eat chocolate. And have sex. They always fix everything.

I tried to always keep these concepts front of mind that winter. I could choose how I thought about anything. If I had to smash out frozen pig poo with an ice pick, instead of cursing and swearing, I would tell myself how much I loved raising pigs, even in winter, how lucky I was to have the strong muscles to swing the axe, and how lucky I was to work outdoors. No matter what I was thinking, I had to deal with the poopsicles regardless, so why whine about it? I was my only audience. I learned to find gratitude in everything, and then focus on that.

I even learned (through a LOT of hard work) to be grateful for your death. Because I lost you, I learned what is really important. I learned what really matters. I now find the beauty in everything. I also remember to realize that no matter how crappy my day is, someone is always having a worse day than me. It's all about perspective.

I would find so much gratitude as well all those nights I would go outside, after the kids had gone to bed and I would sit and enjoy the peace and quiet. I think that's why I always do my best work at night, when the day has finally wound down. No more emails to answer, no more people to manage. Just me and the night sky, which seemed to go on forever. It always grounds me, and reminds me to think big, that anything is possible.

I was working 5 – 6 hours a day at Rhonda's, as well as getting our workshops together, improving the website overall, posting daily, doing farm chores, keeping the house going and trying to keep the kids happy. I was stretched a little thin, as was Chris. It being winter he was working 100 hour weeks, on top of a ton of farm work, and somehow always making the time to be a great Dad. The man blows me away.

And speaking of wind, one afternoon, before we started farming, I was coming down the driveway from work and something looked different about the house, but I couldn't quite figure out what it was. It was only when I pulled right in front of the garage that I realized what had happened.

The carport - now the meat shop, which at that time didn't have a front on it, just wasn't there anymore. Apparently the wind was so strong that it picked the whole thing up – framing, siding, metal roof and all and blew it about 100' into the back yard! Everything inside the carport was left exactly where it was, as if nothing had ever happened. Weird eh?

Another time, on Chris' birthday we woke up to no power. No problem, until I looked out the window and saw that all the neighbours had power. Odd. I went outside and saw that two of the telephone poles on the driveway had completely snapped in half in the storm during the night, and the live wires were just swinging around. Good times.

One Saturday afternoon Chris and the four kids were home. He came running in and tells me that I have to watch out the kitchen window, the one facing the road. All the snow had blown off Lake Louise and it was almost a perfectly flat surface. He had taken a sled, somehow mounted a big stick and was going to tie a tarp to it and make a sail. Hannah was going to be the first test rider.

As I was watching, he hooked up the sail and she began FLYING across the field Mom! Chris took off like a bat out of hell, but really, how fast can you go with a pile of winter clothes on. He couldn't catch up, running as fast as he could and then he totally wiped out. It was pretty funny. When Hannah got to the end of the cleared part, which only took about 6 seconds she landed in a big pile of fluffy snow. Not hurt at all, I could see her smile from the window as she fell over laughing. I think we all thought it was a great idea, but to save it for a less windy day.

We broke a record for most days in a row below minus 20 degrees Celsius the winter of 2013/2014. It was completely ridiculous. I have to say too Mom, with regards to winter, does it ever tick me off when people whine about how bad the roads are. They have absolutely no idea how hard people are working to keep them safe, and how much time they are sacrificing away from their families. Chris hasn't been home for Christmas day in five years now; as fate would have it he's always needed on the roads. And again, the man never complains. So much goodness in him.

Our kids normally love being outside for hours but that winter was so cold they would only last about twenty minutes, and I couldn't blame them. I did my best to make time for playing with them inside, which was tricky with so much else to do. Luckily they were great at coming up with games to play together, which usually involved a lot of running around and lots of high pitched shrieking, my favourite.

The best game I came up with that winter was the "Cooking Game". They'd each lie down on a blanket, them being the main course. If their fate was a taco I'd throw green, red and orange dishtowels on them for toppings. If they were to become banana bread I'd spread chocolate chips – really brown, beige and black face cloths over them. I'd then roll them up as tightly (and safely) as I could in the blanket, with their head sticking out and put them "in the oven", which meant on the couch.

I'd set a digital timer where they could see it and countdown the numbers together. It was usually for 3-5 minutes and they'd spend it making bubbling and cooking noises. It was heaven, sheer bliss not having to worry if they were going to hurt themselves or kill each other, and I could actually take a minute to sit down. Of course I set up pillows on the floor next to the couch, in case they wiggled themselves off into a face plant.

I am a fun Mom but I know I must seem like a real hard ass to other parents. I am extremely strict and have high expectations of our kids, just like you did for us. You screw up – fine, but own it, and if you lie about it, you'll be in more trouble for lying than for whatever you did. This was such an important lesson you taught me, and one we really want our kids to 'get'.

One day, a few years ago one of the boys had a friend over and I overheard him tell the boys that his parents (us) were 'idiots'. That didn't go over too well with me so I called the boy to come downstairs for a 'chat'. I could hear him standing at the top of the stairs talking with our boys, who were saying to him, "Whatever you do, don't lie. She'll know, she always knows. Just be honest and hope for the best." Love those kids.

The long hours, cold winter weather and unending farm chores were definitely taking their toll on us, the animals too. The cattle started losing weight with the extreme cold, so we brought in the vet. He reassured us that it wasn't just us, the cold was affecting all cattle he saw. As per his advice we started supplementing them with a little grain. Wow, did they ever love that, we called it their 'cow crack'.

When the vet was here we had them all 'preg' checked, so we'd know around what time they'd all be due. Turns out half the cows that were supposed to be pregnant had self-aborted with the cold weather. Crap. Totally threw off our breeding plan.

But no matter how cold that winter was, I had something amazing to keep me going, a plane ticket to take off in January to B.C. for a week.

Remember my first trip to B.C. at 19 Mom? I have had the travel bug ever since. I promised myself after that that every two years I would travel somewhere alone and to this day I have stood by it. Maybe it sounds selfish but I make absolutely no apologies for it. I work hard taking care of everything and everyone; I need to take time for me now again. Don't worry Mom; I always stay with friends and fly on Visa points so it hardly costs anything. The one benefit of dumping stuff on a credit card.

I think one of the biggest gifts that travelling has given me is that I just don't place much importance on "stuff" anymore. So many people nowadays seem to be concerned with having "stuff", the latest and the greatest. It's like your social standing is based on how much stuff you have. You know that has never been me. The less I have, the less I have to worry about taking care of. I only want what I need.

I still remember my first trip abroad, and having only one pair of shorts for three months. Poor Wendy, having to look at them every single day. You better believe those went in the garbage when I got home. I would undo my button and they would fall to the ground, still with the mold of my butt in them. Gross.

Travelling gave me a whole new sense of people too. Remember that winter I was supposed to live in Scotland but then I found a round trip ticket AND an apartment in Cyprus for 6 weeks for only $500?

When I was there I had rented a scooter and had driven to the top of the highest mountain in the whole country. I met a Cypriot, with no teeth, about 70 years old who couldn't speak a word of English. It didn't matter though, not one bit. I ended up spending three hours with him having dinner and drinking terrible beer, the whole time communicating only through charades. Isn't it funny how some people can talk non-stop but not really say anything, and then others say so much without ever uttering a word? That night has forever stuck in my mind. Good times with good people, that's what life is all about.

Speaking of language, I have made a point myself of learning how to say please and thank you in every language I can. I've even taught the kids what I know too. There's a store in town where I know the clerks speak Arabic. It was pretty cool to see their faces light up the first couple of times the kids would say thank you to them in their native tongue. There are so many ways to make people smile, so many simple, wonderful ways.

It really is true Mom; it is so easy to brighten someone's day with the smallest gesture. I try to do at least three things a day when I go out to make someone smile, whether I see it or not. Things like putting a loonie in someone's almost expired parking meter, helping someone with their groceries, even holding a door open for someone and giving a heartfelt 'you're welcome' when they say thank you. I'm always telling the kids – kindness is contagious, pass it on.

And then of course there is my childlike silliness that easily brings smiles to all. Just yesterday I went for groceries with the kids, and challenged the guy beside me at a red light to a street race. He started laughing as I sat there revving the engine, egging him on – completely ridiculous as I was in the farm truck and he was in a sports car. My favourite thing I think though has to be telling jokes at drive through windows, here's my favourite;

What's invisible and smells like worms?

Bird farts! HA HA HA!

I still make time to go see concerts too. I remember when I was 16 and came downstairs with a bag of clothes and told you, didn't ask you, that I was going to Ohio to see the Grateful Dead. Now that I'm a parent I know how hard that must have been for you. You let me go. Truth be told we both knew you couldn't stop me. I was just a tad hard headed – wonder where I got that from eh? I actually woke up one morning that weekend with a grilled cheese in my pocket. But that's another story…

Remember that one time you came to pick me up from a concert in Stittsville? I was 16, and my friends and I were so covered in mud we had to line your seats with garbage bags before we could sit down. 'Another Roadslide Attraction' they called it. The Tragically Hip was the band, one of my all-time favourites, and I have gone to see them every chance I could since, at least 7 times. Best kick ass Canadian band ever.

The singer, Gord Downey sadly got brain cancer, but he didn't let it slow him down one bit. He had a complete frontal lobotomy, and then decided to do one more tour across Canada! Tickets were sold out in less than a minute for the Ottawa Show, I didn't have a chance. Dana called me one night and asked what my plans were. I told her how I had a private workshop booked, to start in a couple of hours. "I have a free Hip ticket" was all she said.

I phoned my customer. At first I was going to come up with some lame "I'm sick" excuse, but then of course I couldn't lie, I never could. I told her my real motive for cancelling, and she said, "You better get your butt to that concert and have a great time!" Done.

Mom, what a show!!! It wasn't just the music; it was the feeling that hung in the air. We all realized the significance of the show, it was the end of an era, and the feeling of love and appreciation was absolutely incredible. And even with all he had been through, Gord and the band still rocked the house. There wasn't a dry eye when they took their last bow. I was so lucky to be there, such a great night.

So back to that winter of 2014 and how the cold had somehow gotten even colder by February. I decided to post on Facebook summing up what a jerk winter was being for Canadian Farmers. I wasn't advertising anything in particular, I just wanted to remind people that when they were in their cozy slippers under a blanket, farmers were braving the cold and busy fighting with frozen everything.

It read something along the lines of "-42 degrees today. We are freezing our butts off providing your animals with fresh hay, dry bedding and unfrozen water. Buy local." It was a picture of our cows at a round feeder in the field with the wind so strong the snow was blowing horizontal. So many people "shared" it, which means that now all of their "friends" on Facebook would see it too even if they hadn't 'liked' our page. In the end thousands of people saw the post. Totally crazy Mom, how fast stuff can fly across social media nowadays. You have to be very careful with what you post too; different people interpret things in different ways.

It was pretty funny Mom, as I'd sit in bed brainstorming ideas for different posts about the importance of unplugging, getting off all devices and just enjoying the beauty of here and now. Of course I would do this with my laptop in my lap, my tablet open nearby with music ready for break time, the T.V. on mute and my phone nearby in case the school called. Oh, the irony.

I also spent many, many nights that winter by the fire, knitting with a cat on my lap and listening to videos of different people talking about the power of thought, the universe and the Law of Attraction. And I don't mean just anybody, but people who obviously had their lives together. People like Will Smith, Jim Carrey and Denzel Washington, to name a few.

Finally winter came to an end. I now had a totally new outlook on life. I was marrying everything I had learned about positive thinking, the subconscious and neuroplasticity into a big ol' pot of happy thoughts. My mind was in such a great place Mom. The best feeling was going into the spring knowing that all of our veggies were pre-sold, as were most of our meats.

Chapter 6

"Strive not to be a success, but rather to be of value."

- Albert Einstein

What Blinded Me

The spring and summer of 2014 is when we really started rockin' and rollin'. I had finished my house cleaning and was excited about the season ahead. The workshops were ready to go. We were ready for the veggie and meat CSA programs to start. We'd found a new butcher who cut, wrapped, labelled and priced every meat package just how we wanted. No more dinky scale and hand stamping, and it looked a heck of a lot more professional too.

We knew we needed more hands on the farm. Chris and I had hummed and hawed about whether we should pay someone full time or host someone from abroad. We first thought of converting the attic into a cool space for someone but then decided against it. It was enough having strangers around all the time, we didn't want one in our home. We'd just bite the bullet and pay someone.

We had sent out a job posting and ended up interviewing a guy named Cory, a big bearded bald redhead. I was in the middle of a job when he showed up. He grabbed a nearby shovel and began helping me as we talked. In my mind he was hired right then and there.

He ended up staying for two hours and helped me with a whole bunch of stuff. We had a great time together. I even threw in a few of my stupid jokes to test the waters. He laughed and threw in a few of his own. I farted by accident and he didn't bat an eyelash. This was definitely someone I could spend my days working alongside. He started a couple of weeks later.

The chickens, turkeys and ducks were now free ranging all over the Farm, dropping their 'landmines' wherever they wanted. I had to be conscious of bringing poop near any food, so I introduced a 'barefoot only' rule in the garden. Instead of fencing off the animals, we fenced off all the gardens. So glad you always taught me to think outside the box Mom, it always opens up a world of solutions.

I remember coming out to the garden that spring to find William showing a customer around. He was doing a great Vanna White, showcasing all of our veggies. The lady was quite an older lady, holding her wee purse, short white hair, matching lilac jacket and skirt suit, and nylons with … no shoes. Apparently he wouldn't let her in until she took her loafers off. Love that boy.

Cory was a really hard worker and so much fun to work with Mom. We laughed all day together. One afternoon we were working, I had my head down weeding and I hear him holler from across the garden – "Hey, what's this bug?" I turn around only to be blinded by a flash of white light. It was his butt - he was mooning me! I instantly dropped to my knees I was laughing so hard. Good times.

The kids were also a huge help in the garden too. They were great at seeding, their adorable pudgy little fingers gently plopping the seeds into the rows, carefully checking with me every now and then to make sure they were doing it right. They were happy to help weed and absolutely loved helping us harvest. It was so great to have them see the whole process, from start to finish and learn where food really comes from. It was also a heck of a lot easier to get them to eat veggies when they had grown them themselves.

That summer your poor wee grandbabies had their first puke-fest. They had each only vomited one time before then, which was pretty good considering they were now 6 and 7.

They were 2 and 3 years old the very first time they ever threw up. They were only sick once, the whole thing only lasting about 6 seconds each. Mom, they had the absolute best reactions. The first one threw up hours after dinner, looked at me and said, "I ate too much Mommy, so I had to spit some out." The second one threw up not five minutes later, looked at me with this totally confused look and said, "My supper was in my mouth again."

Neither of them shed a tear or complained. I acted like it was no big deal, and so did they.

Somehow that summer Cory was there they had both gotten a bug. I set up a mattress in the living room, and they got to watch T.V. all day long. I tried to make it fun for them, and set up a little 'vomit' scoreboard. They were happy every time their number went up, so at least it kept them smiling. They were good about drinking water, I was careful to keep them hydrated but they only ate one cracker each the whole day. It was so weird Mom, I had never seen them like that.

Even though they were so sick they were still the most pleasant little people ever, and kept thanking me for all the kisses and cuddles. One thing I have to say about our munchkins Mom, they are really good about just going with the flow and rolling with whatever life brings them. Truth be told it was wonderful not having to chase them for a day. Of course they were back to themselves the next day, running and playing. I think they ate everything in the house.

Cory and I soon had our system for weeding, watering and harvesting. Katie would show up every Tuesday and Friday to pick up all the harvested veggies to deliver. Everything ran so smoothly, it was so great to finally have a proper commercial garden.

Katie also introduced me to the National Farmers Union, a group of small scale Canadian farmers working together towards common goals. I started going to meetings and getting more involved. I loved that it was run by a group of farmers, working for farmers. It was so nice to be able to talk about my job with people that weren't the general public. People who really got what it is like to farm, not just the fun stuff but all the really hard stuff too.

A few months later I became a Director for our Local Chapter of the NFU, (I'm now the secretary) which gave me voting rights and the chance to make a real difference for all Canadian small scale farms just like ours. Such a great organization, made up of such genuine of people, doing really important work. I was really proud to be a part of it all.

Come late winter I was really excited and pretty nervous the morning of my first workshop. I had gone through it in front of a mirror a couple of times; feeling like an idiot talking to myself but whatever, it helped a lot. I had everything planned out perfectly, except for the surprise spring blizzard that happened the day before...

The morning of the workshop I mapped out the garden beds with stakes and string lines – in the snow! I set up a little amphitheatre of hay bales in the garage and taught in there. Luckily a friend had brought a huge pot of hot chocolate for everyone. The people in the group were real troopers in the cold, and I think they all learned a lot. First workshop done. I was nervous, and I did it. I was learning to be comfortable being uncomfortable.

The following week I gave the same workshop to a different group – this time in the house. The kids were as usual bouncing off the walls that morning. One jumped so hard he broke the couch, so now one end was sitting on the ground. This was 20 minutes before people were meant to arrive. I quickly grabbed some tools and fixed it, or so I thought...

Of course, the couch broke again when the first person sat on it. I was mortified. I retold the story of our son's trampoline act. Everyone had a good laugh and I gave the workshop with three wonderful people sitting on the now cleverly named "couch ramp".

I had an hour between the morning and afternoon workshops, so I scrambled and fixed it again. Second group arrives; someone sits on the couch and it breaks again. I retold them the story, as if it was the first time and taught a second group with the couch ramp in effect. I was embarrassed but no one seemed to mind. I think most of them were parents and agreed that kids do silly things at the worst possible times, and you just have to laugh.

I know you know what I mean Mom, when you are trying to be professional and your kids mess it up. I remember when you were holding a meeting in the kitchen, I think with some bigwigs from Toronto. I was smoking a joint on the second story balcony right above you, and all the smoke, unbeknownst to me just kept blowing right in the kitchen. Sorry about that! Speaking of which, recreational marijuana use is supposedly meant to be legalized this year – Oct. 20, 2018. I'll wait and see if it really happens. Fingers crossed.

We started our meat CSA in April of 2014. It definitely took a few months to get into the swing of weighing out everybody's shares and keeping the freezers organized. I would do the CSA deliveries once a month to town to set locations, no more home deliveries.

By the end of the summer I still had some pork in the freezer that had to get gone. We were growing more than needed for CSA's but farm gate sales hadn't cleaned us out as I had hoped. Now with the program running, I refused to put anything on sale as it wouldn't be fair to those who had signed up for a year with us and were paying top dollar.

One day I was chatting with a volunteer at the Opportunity Shop in Arnprior. Yes Mom I still shop there, two bucks for jeans – how can you go wrong? It turns out she also helped out with a local Church food program, helping people down on their luck.

I went to the Church the next day with two big bags of pork. A beautiful, kind hearted, round lady with rosy cheeks met me at the door. Her eyes welled up with tears when I gave her the donations. It was an incredible feeling for me, knowing how much it would help, really help people. Everybody deserves a full belly. I decided right then and there that twice a year I would donate to those in need.

Some might say I should always be making every penny I can, but the feeling I get from helping people who need it is priceless. I remember growing up, we didn't have tons of money but you always found some to donate when you could. You taught me that's what life is about, help when you can. In the beginning I would post about the generosity, but then I stopped. I wasn't doing it for a pat on the back; I was doing it because it was the right thing to do. "Well done is better than well said" as Ben Corylin put it.

And truth be told, you never know when you may need help too. I remember you saying those exact words to me when I was about 12 and Joan from Kinburn came to the door canvassing for Cancer. Just a tad ironic looking back. The first year we moved back to the Farm after you left, I became a team leader for Cancer canvassing in Kinburn. We didn't have lots of money to give, but I was happy to give my time.

Calving went really well that spring – everybody came out and stood up and had a drink. Phew. By midsummer business was going so well that we had eaten everybody we could. There were meant to be more moo moos ready for the spa but with the self-aborting crap from two years earlier our numbers were down. We bought a whole bunch of cows from Fred across the road. I knew how he raised them, treated them and what he fed them. All the feed and bedding coming from either our farm or his. You can't get more local or sustainable than that.

I added a disclaimer to our website that sometimes we buy cows from other farmers. I wanted to be completely transparent. We had now gained the trust of our community and in our product. We had even converted a couple of vegetarians, and I didn't take that lightly. I hardly ate meat for years for ethical reasons, so I needed to honour theirs.

They were a different breed then our Herefords, more jumpy and totally unpredictable. Their arrival brought about the standard initial butt sniff greetings, and then everyone decided to get along.

A few days later we brought the herd up from the field and put them in the big section of the barn. We were just letting them settle down for a bit before we started sorting them. I would be in charge of closing the gate once we had separated the ones we needed to into another pen.

This one cow, one of Fred's cows, took off as if she was on speed and started running circles in the barn. I was standing in a corner, minding my own business, letting her get all of her silliness out when she circled right close to me, kicking me in the thigh on her way by – hard enough to drop me like a ton of bricks. We started calling her "Crazy Bitch" after that.

A short while later we started sorting them. Most of them easily went into the pen we wanted. Crazy bitch was almost through the gate that I was about to close when she did a sideways jump, throwing her weight into the gate and smashing it into my face. The top bar hit my nose so hard I was sure it was broken. Lucky thing she was pregnant or I would have set up a Spa date for her that afternoon. I had absolutely no interest in having an animal on the farm that would hurt someone.

That summer we got some other furry friends as well, two surprise horses for Hannah. We told her there was a new calf in the barn and to come check it out. When she slid open the door Mom, the look on her face was totally awesome. Her smile went from ear to ear and she couldn't stop giggling. I am all about surprises and that one was definitely one of the best ones ever.

Turned out one of the two horses was a little strange though, always looking at you with the sideways eye ball. One day Chris and I decided to go for a ride and he got on the weirdo, following behind me on my horse. Two seconds later I heard a yelp only to see his horse go flying by, with only Chris's boot left in the stirrup. I turned around and the poor guy was still skidding on the ground from his high speed fall.

He got back on, and stayed on for the next few minutes. Then Brody, the weirdo, went totally nuts and started bucking, sending Chris once again through the air. He opted this time not to get back on. Don't blame him – Brody was nuts!

We called the trainer we got him from and sent him back to get calmed down a bit. She called me about a week later and said she had something to tell me that was going to sound completely bananas. She was right.

When a friend of hers, another trainer was over, they both had a look at him. Now I didn't see it with my own eyes Mom, but this is what she told me. Her friend shot her a funny look and then held a hose over Brody's back and very, very faint black stripes started to show up. Apparently way back in the lineage a zebra and horse had got it on, and the by–product of their happy times was a 'zorse' – half zebra half horse, which is why he was so nuts. We told her thank you very much for your honesty, and that we didn't want him back.

I needed to get even more people interested in the Farm, with the plan next year being to double our CSA meat shares. I came up with a few ideas. First we had a 'Family Fun Farm Day'. It was all about letting kids be kids and get as muddy as they could.

There was tons of fun stuff to do – bean bag toss, potato sack races, egg on a spoon obstacle courses, it was great. Lots of people showed up and we sold a pile of meat. It was a lot to organize, and thankfully we had a bunch of volunteers helping us out. It was a huge success. I knew both the parents and their kids would remember the fun they had on our Farm.

I wanted to get people more involved on-line with our Farm too. I held a contest on Facebook to see who could come up with the best "veggie face". I remember how much fun we had as kids making them with stuff from your Mom's garden. It was a total flop; we didn't get even one entry. I sucked it up, created my own veggie face, called Auntie C to let her know what was coming and announced her as the winner, and thanked everyone for their great entries. No use having a pity party, on to the next idea.

We then had a "Find the Farmer" contest. Cory and I had a blast taking the 'Where's Waldo' pics of me on the farm. It worked, and really got people involved on-line. I didn't realize until I was posting them that in one photo I was hiding behind the herd way off in a field, with just my head showing. The angle though made it look like my head was coming out of a cow's butt!

I had been reading more and more about the Law of Attraction and manifesting throughout the spring and it still sounded kind of hokey to me. 'Just picture what you want and see it as already yours. Doesn't matter how you are going to get it, just know that you will.' I had to try it out. I had to see with my own eyes if it really happened, if it was really possible. Being a science nerd, I needed hard core proof.

We have this beautiful park bench under the lilac tree by the garage, the one that used to be on the balcony where I would…enjoy life in my teen years. It needed 'some lipstick' on the sides as your Mom would have said; big flower planters would be perfect. I decided these would be what I would manifest.

I started to consciously feel gratitude for these big beautiful planters that would just happen into our laps. I visualized them showing up and planting them. It was really a weird exercise, but I gave it 100%. Even though they weren't here yet, I thought as if it was a done deal that they were coming. Same way as if I had ordered them on-line and was just waiting for their delivery.

I kid you not Mom, three days after I started "manifesting" them, Chris called me from work. I hadn't said a word to him about what I was trying to do. He said he had found two planters on the side of the road left out for the garbage, and that he'd bring them home for me.

They were massive, at least two feet tall with the same width, and I'm sure at least eighty bucks each brand new. Well holy moly. It was weird, and yet not surprising somehow.

Okay, this could just be a total fluke I thought. I had to push it even more. I now needed something to put in these planters. I did the same exercise with manifesting plants to fill them. Feeling the gratitude of having beautiful free plants fall in my lap, visualizing me filling the planters with soil and putting in the plants.

Two days later Cory and I were sitting on the bench having lunch and he asks me what the big black ball was way out in the front hay field. I had no idea, so I hiked all the way out to it. It was a huge root ball of a rhubarb plant, with the green leaves starting to grow out of it. ARE YOU FREAKIN KIDDING ME? No way would I ever have thrown out rhubarb, and if I ever did it would have gone to the pigs. To this day I have no idea how it got there, but you better believe that I knew in the moment I had the power to make things happen. The planters had me intrigued; the rhubarb sealed the deal. Interesting…

We had a daily routine of animal chores - checking hay, water, fence lines, for cuts or scrapes on the animals or anything out of the ordinary. Or at least I thought I had...

I did chores one morning, came in and Chris had to run out to the barn for something soon after. He came in and nonchalantly said to me, "So, you didn't happen to notice the dead cow during chores?" Turns out it was Rocky, he had bloated. Bloat is essentially when the cow's lower abdomen keeps filling up with air, much like a balloon that doesn't stop inflating. Crap.

He bloated from eating too much alfalfa too quickly, in its immature stage before it flowered. With the drought the previous year, many of our pasture grasses and other legumes had died off and there was more alfalfa than usual. When it has flowered, the cell walls thicken making it harder to digest, so cows eat it more slowly. But we had moved them too soon into a new pasture. The alfalfa was very succulent and juicy and the cows loved it, chowing it down way too fast to have enough time to properly digest it. They couldn't burp out the gasses fast enough, and bloating was the result. Exactly how the hell were we supposed to know that? Lesson learned, move on.

Once we figured out what had happened after a panicked call to Fred, we had to get the rest of the herd moving, and fast, to get all their burps out. I hopped on the four wheeler, Chris was on foot and we moved them back to the initial pasture with less alfalfa. We just kept moving them around for an hour until we were sure there wasn't any chance of anybody else bloating.

Definitely one of those lessons that would have been much easier NOT to learn the hard way. Rocky was booked for the Spa in a few weeks, so that was incredibly frustrating. The meat was absolutely fine, but an animal has to walk into an abattoir to be processed, bottom line. So all that meat was wasted and we lost a LOT of money. Find the rainbow – at least it was only one cow right?

We needed to replace him, right quick. Nobody else was ready to cross Rainbow Bridge, and I needed beef in the freezer. We bought a grass fed steer, the friendliest steer I had ever met. I called him "Buddy". He'd come and stand right beside me, gently leaning his neck on my side, politely asking for scratches.

He was booked to go to the Spa in a month. About three weeks after we got him I noticed him walking and it looked like his back legs were drunk. His whole backend would gently fall to the side as if his legs had fallen asleep. He would get up and take a couple of steps and it would happen again. Luckily the last time he went down it was in the barn on a nice batch of fresh straw. I brought him some hay and a bucket of water. I called the vet.

The vet came and started assessing him. He couldn't figure out what it was, nothing was apparent - no broken bones in his legs or hips, he didn't have a fever, it was a total mystery. One possibility that he couldn't rule out was rabies. Hearing that word made me sick to my stomach because while waiting on the vet I had sat down with Buddy, his head in my lap and was feeding him hay and getting slobber all over my hands, which were of course full of cuts.

He didn't get any better by the next night and he now had absolutely no feeling in his back end. If a cow can't walk, they can't eat. Damn. We had to make the call. The only way to know the cause of death for sure would be to send him for a full autopsy, which would be free of charge to us. Even if we did have to pay we would have had it done, we wanted to know what happened.

Turns out Buddy had a broken spine. I don't know if he had slipped, or if someone had jumped on his back or what had happened. Either way, it didn't matter, the whole thing was horrible. This poor guy lost his life, and we lost a pile of money buying him and now had the vet bill too. And the fact that we had lost two animals so close together was pretty hard. At least I didn't have rabies right? There was always a bright side if I looked for it.

In every other way the season was wrapping up nicely. I had learned so much from Katie that season and was so grateful for her patience for all my questions. She was so great to work with, always complimenting how great all the veggies looked when she picked them up. You'd laugh Mom, we were growing so many veggies that you tried to make us eat as kids, that I still don't like even though I have tried them again over the years. Things like rutabaga and turnips. Blech!

That fall we were feeding 20 families our veggies and 20 families our meats, some of them in both CSA programs would buy our eggs too. We were really doing what we set out to do.

It was so great to have Cory around too because it meant I had someone to have lunch with. This must sound ridiculous to you Mom, I know how much you loved being in the kitchen. Remember how I can't stand cooking Mom? Same thing goes for eating. Being a workaholic I find it hard to make myself take the time to eat something more than an apple or a banana when I'm alone.

Thing is when I don't eat, I get weak. When I get weak, I have more anxiety which makes me sick to my stomach and then I don't want to eat at all. And I spent ALL DAY around good food! How totally messed up is that? Thank goodness for Cory, he was a great cook and always happy to whip something up for lunch. Full belly, happy thoughts.

What felt so good too was that when Cory started he mentioned how he was thinking about moving to B.C. By the time he ended the season with us, he bought a plane ticket; he had decided to take the leap. It felt great thinking that maybe him listening to me yammer all summer about believing in yourself encouraged him to decide. There's nothing better than seeing people going after what they want.

So all in all the spring and summer of 2014 was a huge success. Both our CSA programs were working out really well, and with Cory's extra hands we had a lot more time with the kids. Sales were increasing, and our reach was getting further. It felt amazing.

Family picture, the kids were 9 and 10

Stella

Blueberry

The Meat Shop the first year

Taking down the building

The barn we traded for beer

Farmher pose

Chris building the cow barn

The cow barn all finished!

The new garden

Katie and I

My clothes after saving the septic calf   The boys out front

Dave the Duck…   Kitchen counter kitty

Baby quackers

The boys and their sheep   Big date at a farm auction

Chris and I loving life   Walter the cow dog

Home Sweet Home

Chapter 7

"Whatever makes you uncomfortable is your biggest opportunity for growth."

- Bryant McGill

Found Just What We Needed

The spring and summer of 2014 were amazing; Katie, Cory and I had a real blast working together. We planted over 25,000 seeds, fed a lot of people and my back and shoulder definitely felt it. I was looking forward to the colder months and becoming a computer geek once again.

Our main goals for the coming fall and winter were to improve our marketing strategy even more, get some publicity and find workers for the next season.

Stepping up marketing was a no brainer. I needed to cement my butt in front of the computer and learn everything I could. I had to start thinking outside the box.

What emotions do different colours trigger? What font size is most effective on graphics? What graphics were most appealing? Where is the most effective to place text on a graphic? How many words are just enough but not too many? How many milliseconds does it take for someone to decide to actually read the post? What basics do you need to grab that attention? How to create trust with your posts? How pushy is too pushy?

Like I said Mom, the internet is now so mind boggling. You can find anything on it. I found answers to all these questions, which led to so many more. Learning the psychology behind marketing was absolutely fascinating to me. It all goes back to what has been stored in our subconscious mind. Without being consciously aware of it, our gut feeling tells us if something makes us feel good or not.

When some parts of the brain are triggered, it gives out a little shot of dopamine – 'the happy drug'. That is why we sometimes automatically associate happy feelings with some products, even though we have never tried them before. They have been marketed in a way that taps into information stored in our brain we aren't even aware of. Even things as simple as colours – red and yellow being the ones most associated with hunger. Kind of makes sense when you look at logos for McDonalds and Wendy's. Pretty cool stuff, but also kind of scary that we can so easily be manipulated without even knowing it.

I took all the information I had learned and integrated it into how we were posting. It was great to have more of an in-depth understanding, and be more intentional with how our posts were put together. I definitely noticed an increase in our 'engagement' – people interacting by clicking an emoji or leaving a comment, and also with sales.

And I realized something about myself too Mom that surprised me: I really, really enjoyed all the computer stuff. I love figuring out how to make things work. Who would have thought a tie-dyed hippy girl would love working on a computer so much eh?

I had to put on my big girl pants to increase our publicity. Speaking in front of people intimidates the heck out of me but it's what I needed to do. By now I was used to being uncomfortable. I sent out emails to local radio stations, television stations and newspapers telling them about us, and how our upcoming workshops would make a great feature story. I didn't hear back for a while from any of them, which I was fine with. I was working on simply 'trusting it would all work out'.

The Ottawa Citizen contacted us a little while later and we set up a time for an interview. I was excited but also really nervous too. I knew the potential reach it would have for us, so I just hiked up those pants a little higher. I had to believe in myself.

The writer came and we did the interview over coffee. I had now told "our story" so many times I knew to focus on the parts that people always found most interesting. She asked great questions and seemed genuinely impressed with our story; it was a real compliment to me. This lady gets to meet all kinds of amazing people doing incredible things, and here she was enjoying herself with little ol' me.

The day the photographer came to do the shoot for the article the temperature was minus three hundred. Okay, well not really that cold, but it was bloody freezing. I had snow plowed the driveway for her but not five minutes later the winds had blown in and created a drift at the corner right by the house. That drift is my nemesis Mom; thankfully she steamed through it with her car no problem.

At the barn she started taking a bunch of shots of me and the cows, always with a huge smile on my face. Only problem was it was so cold my teeth kept turning into frozen chicklets. The shoot was soon done, I thanked her a million times for braving the cold and she headed off. It felt great to have it done, and I was really excited to see the article.

A couple of weeks later I was wasting time on Facebook and got a notification that Wendy had mentioned my name - "So proud of my friend Katrina and this amazing article about their business" with a link to our article in the Citizen. It was awesome – a full page article!

In the next couple of weeks I kept getting messages from friends and family congratulating us on it. A lot of those people were the same ones who said we could never do it in the beginning. Ha! Also, all of our workshops sold out instantly and I even had to add a few more dates. I was on cloud nine. I had just trusted, and it had worked. As soon as I stopped worrying about when we'd get more publicity, really stopped worrying about it, it landed right in our lap.

Then Lisa's wonderful hubby called from Montreal, out of the blue asking if he could come and shoot some Go Pro videos of our farm for our YouTube Channel. You betcha! The day he showed up was another really cold day. He was such a trooper. We shot for about an hour.

At one point, when we were filming the pig segment, I had the camera strapped around my waist. Out of nowhere a pig, almost full grown at this point, decides to barrel in between my legs and go for the food trough. She was so round that when she went through my legs she actually lifted me up off my feet and I ended up riding her for a few steps. Good times. It still makes me chuckle when I watch it.

We were then contacted by Lightchasers Photography, an amazing local couple who wanted to feature us in an article. Nicest people ever. They came out, thankfully it wasn't too cold, and we had a nice walk about, chatting and taking pictures. Their article was so flattering, the way she spoke about our Farm and how she had heard about what we were doing and just had to meet us. The photos of the animals were incredible too; it is always nice to see the beauty of things you take for granted, through someone else's eyes.

My head was in such a great place Mom. Tom had nothing to bug me about, and his silence was such a blessing. I wasn't worrying about everything we had to get done, I was just trusting it would all fall into place. It really was true – the more things I had gratitude for, the more things showed up to be grateful for.

One thing I started doing around this time too was changing the way I would compliment people. I used to say something nice to someone, and then often watch them stumble to find a response and it would be awkward. I don't know when people started feeling weird with kindness, but I found a way to fix it.

Now I don't give people a chance to respond after I compliment them, I'll just wait a second to see from their reaction that they've heard it, and then I carry on talking right away. It takes the weirdness of it, and the feeling that they "have" to say something back.

My whole change in attitude and mindset affected every area of my life. It did wonders for my OCD and, 'everything has to be perfect' mindset.

That forgotten plate I found after the kids went to bed, that once would have sent me reeling – now I saw it differently. It showed me that they took it upon themselves to fix their own snack.

The never ending laundry that always needed to be done – how lucky were we to have so many clothes to keep us warm?

The never ending pile of dishes – it showed me how fortunate we were to have all that good food to eat.

And as soon as I started watching what language I was using, it became so easy to be positive about everything. It was all about my perspective. Any sentence I went to say that had a 'can't' or 'won't', I'd just switch it around in my head.

I can't wait to go to the store – I'll be so glad when I get to the store.

I don't want to be late – I'll leave early to be sure to be on time.

I don't think it will fit – I'll see if I can move something to make it work.

One of the biggest changes in my thinking came when I stopped saying "I have to" and "I should", in my head as well as when I spoke. Of course there were still things that needed to be done, but when I changed how I phrased it all of a sudden it didn't sound so bad, I would even look forward to it.

Instead of "I have to clean out the chicken coop" I'd say "The chickens will be so happy when I get their house cleaned up."

"I have to go get pig food" would become "I'll be glad to have lots of feed and not worry about running out."

I changed the way I thought about "should". Either I was going to or I wasn't, plain and simple. Using should somehow implied guilt if I didn't get it done, and I didn't want to be saying anything that had any negative connotations to it.

Or, instead of 'have to' or 'should', I would say 'I am'. I am going to clean the coop. I am going to call Auntie. I am going to check the fencer. Just those little changes made the difference in how I thought about things – now there weren't feelings of obligation or maybe even dread – it was all related to action.

One really neat thing that happened that summer Mom was that we sent some meat up to Iqaluit. That's a pretty cool delivery from a wee town named Kinburn. The logistics weren't too bad; we just had to *figure it out*. And the customer LOVED our meats, which was great to hear.

It had been great having Cory for the summer, but it was a real kick in the pants financially. We were at the end of our rope with trying to balance work and having the kids home all summer. It became pretty clear that the next year we needed two extra sets of hands all summer, and not just for 9 – 5 Monday to Friday.

We revisited the idea of having people live here. The only way it would work was if they had a separate house. As luck would have it, right around that time, a friend of ours asked us if we knew anybody who needed a big trailer, the kind that's really a house and stays parked on a site permanently.

Are you kidding me? What perfect timing for that to land right in our laps. I had to check the sky and make sure I didn't see pigs flying by.

We bought it and parked it by the coverall. It was so nice Mom - hard wood flooring, a full kitchen, air conditioning, heat, a surround sound stereo, two bunk beds in one bedroom, a queen size bed in the other, tons of closet space, a pull out couch in the living room and a great bathroom. It would be perfect for two people, with enough space to not be on top of each other. It suited our needs to a tee.

We decided we wanted to host international people. I have such great memories of my farm stays in Australia, and I was thrilled to be able to give that experience to people travelling around Canada. I remember all the great people who helped you guys out when we were growing up. I knew what a great experience it would be for the kids to meet people from a different culture, who could speak a different language and cooked different foods. We were pretty grounded on the farm. Why not bring the world to us right? Thinking outside the box.

I know enough about travelling to know that anybody who has their life together enough to sort out visas, tickets and save their pennies would be very responsible, and make great workers. It didn't matter if they had any farm experience, I'd teach them. What mattered was that they were happy to do anything we asked, and that they fit well into our family.

We made a profile on Help X and Work Away, two sites that connect volunteers and those people who need help. We plugged in our timeline, what their duties would be, and a little bit about the farm. We needed them to be over 25, be available May – Oct and not be a vegetarian. I respect anyone's food choices, but I am not about to make separate meals for people. We got a few replies but none of them really fit. I started sending messages privately to people who looked fun.

I ended up setting up Skype interviews with two ladies, one from Belgium and one from Australia, in the same week. 'Skype' Mom, is like a chat you have with someone on the computer, where you can both see each other talking. It is the best way to see what someone is like, really like. Anyone can sound great on paper, but if someone was going to be part of our family, I wanted to see their energy. I liked the two ladies right away. They were both bubbly and full of enthusiasm.

I had four questions ready, the same four we have asked everybody since.

1) Are you fine with helping cook dinner?
2) Are you fine with helping out with the kids?
3) Do you have any allergies?
4) We like beer, a lot. Is this a problem for you?

I wasn't trying to be funny for that last one but I always wanted to be upfront about it. It's cool if people don't drink and don't want to be around anyone that does, but I had to let them know this would definitely not be the place for that.

After a couple more chats with each of the ladies, they signed our Letter of Offer and we sealed the deal. The first listed duty on the letter was making weeknight dinners. I built it in so that I didn't have to cook as much. We would do a meal plan together on Sunday based on what was in the house and ready in the garden, and then I'd go pick up whatever else we needed. This would take out the mad panic of last minute meals, thank goodness.

I was so looking forward to having two built-in fun people around. Travellers are happy to do anything, seeing everything as fun because it is all so new. The best thing is getting to see Canada through someone else's eyes, what makes us unique. Things like milk in bags, apologizing profusely and ending every question with EH? And of course Canadian bacon, maple syrup and poutine. Their head always tilts a bit sideways when I explain what it is but then I take them for one at Five Span Spuds in Pakenham (best poutine ever!) and they're hooked.

I could now finally step away a bit from working 'in' the business and spend more time working 'on' it, and most importantly have more time for the kids, real quality time.

How the heck you did it Mom I will never know. You went to school full time, worked full time growing your business and still every meal was homemade, delicious and on the table by 6:00 p.m. I remember every Tuesday night you wouldn't sleep, so you could squeeze another 8 hours into your week. I tried a couple of times to do all-nighters, but those days were long gone for me. I need sleep, not much but some.

You were such an amazing Mom, even those days you hadn't slept. I am sorry that I wasn't nicer to you in my teens. I was too busy with my head up my butt thinking the world revolved around me. I was a real jerk, and I am so sorry. You always made me feel loved though, no matter how terrible I was to you. Moms are like that.

The kids by now had grown out of the whole "cooking" game so I started to teach them card games. It was so cold that winter we stayed in the kitchen as much as we could, enjoying the wood stove. I'd spread a blanket on the floor, make a pile of snacks and we'd sit and play for hours. So great to be able to do with them the exact things I loved to do with you.

I have to admit though, as they grew up a bit more; I missed the games from when they were really small, my favourite one being Hide and Seek. Because I would really play Hide and Don't Seek. I would just keep counting down the numbers, and after a few have my voice trail off. A couple of minutes later I'd count down more, and again trail off. Definitely gave me a few more minutes of peace and quiet. I remember you telling me how you were playing with us once as kids and you waited so long to go looking you found Ryan asleep in a closet.

Business was so great that year, I mean really great – our sales had increased 250% in the past year since working with Angie. She was definitely worth every penny, and then some.

By now all the turkeys had gone to freezer camp and our ducks soon would go too, which made me sad. The ducks have always been my favourite of all the animals on the farm.

One morning while doing chores I found a duck egg. I had never eaten them before and heard they were delicious. I brought it in the house, grabbed a pan, cracked it open and.... felt like the biggest meanie ever. I didn't know the egg had been fertilized; the thought hadn't even crossed my mind. There was a little dude living in there. It took one or two breaths and then went to sleep. I felt like such a jerk Mom. Lesson learned. Move on.

A few days later doing dishes, looking out the window a duck waddles by, with two little fluffy tennis balls following her! So cute. We all went out to see the babies, and the kids discovered another ducking that was half frozen, it was late fall by then. The boys brought it in and Charles held it warmly to his chest in front of the fire. It was the coolest thing ever Mom, watching it thaw and then come to life. An hour later it was completely fine and touring around the kitchen like nobody's business.

I didn't want the duckling to smell too much like us, and have the Mama not take care of him so we brought him back to the duck coop that afternoon, and gave them all lots of cozy bedding.

By now I was getting emails and phone calls from folks looking for advice in all kinds of areas - gardening, raising chickens, starting a business, marketing food – you name it. It felt AMAZING to be recognized as someone who was knowledgeable and friendly enough to be approached. I always made the time to chat with people on the phone, or answer their email as best I could. Nothing feels better than helping people, in any way you can, absolutely nothing.

It was getting very hard to balance work and family. The family came first, always, but the onus of bringing in money weighed on me just as much. It was my decision to leave my steady paycheck, and it was my responsibility to replace that income. We were making great money, but it was going out just as fast as it came in with all the surprise expenses. I know Mom you totally understand how easy it is to hemorrhage money while running a farm. It was pretty much the only thing at that time that was stressing me out, a lot.

More and more I was putting the kids aside to work on the computer building the business and make more money, but it wasn't fair to them.

They didn't want money, they just wanted me. I wasn't making the time I should have for them, and I knew it. I had to make some changes.

That is when I really started recognizing the value of my time, and not feeling bad about spending it wisely. I learned to **say no**. It was hard at first but then I realized – no to this means yes to that. If I was going to make this business work, I had to be saying yes to the right things. I became very intentional with all of my choices. I learned it is not selfish, exactly the opposite actually.

I needed to be less stressed and find more time. I needed to get rid of any household 'lose my mind' triggers. Things like piles of laundry, thrown together meals, lousy school lunches, and our Tupperware drawer from hell. So I created systems to save my sanity and time. I so understand now Mom, why you lived by lists and strict routines with some things – because it gave you so much freedom in others. Works for me!

Even with something as simple as a list I was intentional. The first word was always a verb. The less I had to think, the better. They weren't huge changes to make, but what a difference. I still make the same weekly lists now, three years later. Meal plans and chore charts are the backbone; everyone knows what's coming and what's expected of them. I go into my weeks knowing 'home' will flow smoothly and it's such a huge weight off my shoulders.

I was really tired of nagging the kids ALL THE TIME to do the same stuff every day. We began the kids with their first chore charts then, they were seven and eight at the time. They were old enough to understand the difference between being responsible or being reminded. Slowly, they began doing things without reminders for the treasured red checkmark. Much older now, we have had to resort to cold hard cash. Either way, they have learned the lesson – you want something, you have to work for it. That's life baby.

Also going into the winter that fall of 2014 I knew I wanted the kids to watch less T.V. I had been letting them have a few too many video game marathons. Every night we all did something together for an hour before they went to bed. We'd often lie by the fire and play with the cats. Now with them a little older I taught them how to play crib. Charles turned into an instant superstar at it. At first I was easy on him but then he kept whipping my butt even when I was genuinely trying to kick his.

I thought outside the box when coming up with fun stuff to do. We'd set up a tent in the living room and camp out for the night and cook hot dogs on the woodstove. We'd make massive forts and then watch movies in them with popcorn and flashlights. Thing is with our kids, I think the same goes for a lot of kids, it doesn't matter really what you do with them, the whole thing is to be together. To spend time doing what they like to do.

More gratitude for you in this department Mom. No matter how busy you were, you always made time to do really fun stuff with us. Some of my best childhood memories are building igloos in the backyard, snowmobile picnics or when you'd have us spin the globe, pick somewhere, and then you'd make us a traditional dinner from that country. Hay wagon rides, scavenger hunts and awesome afternoons making Papier Mache, all amazing. Being a parent now, I really, really appreciate all those great times we spent as a family.

Something I did for myself that fall was to do a massive de-clutter. I went through the house top to bottom, and got rid of anything I saw that I hadn't used in a year. This was another great exercise in noticing the "have to's" or "should's" I associated with stuff. I am all for nostalgia, but for me, a messy house makes for a messy head. No thanks.

That fall and winter was the best yet since we started farming. It wasn't too cold, it snowed enough we were grateful for the overtime but Chris wasn't gone 24/7. We had found live-in help for the coming season which would be great on so many different levels. More hands meant Chris and I might actually get to relax a little bit and enjoy each other more. Yes please!

Chapter 8

"True manifesting is letting the universe

catch up with your dreams."

- Gabrielle Bernstein

Me, a Cow Trampoline

We were thrilled when the spring of 2015 came. We had two awesome ladies soon coming to help us, with a beautiful trailer all set up for them. I love Chris and the boys with all my heart but I was definitely looking forward to having a little more estrogen around. Both our annual meat and veggie CSA's were sold out and upcoming workshops were close to full. I was feeling totally unstoppable.

Spring meant new baby ducks, turkeys, and chicks but most importantly our winter pigs would soon be crossing the rainbow bridge. Raising pigs that winter sucked. For some reason they had started pooing in the barn, not outside. This meant every day or two, in my Gumby suit, I had to shovel their heavy, smelly frozen crap into a wheel barrow and then trek it way out into the field through the snow. At least it meant I would have a ton of great meats to sell right?

The stinkin' water hydrant in the barn froze late that winter. So every day, often twice a day I had to fill one of those big blue Culligan water jugs in the bathtub, haul it downstairs and outside, put it on a sled I tied to my waist and then make the trek to the pig barn through the snow. Good times.

The solitude of winter really got to me that year. I knew I had to do something to be around more people. Farming can get pretty darn lonely. The only people outside the family I was seeing were customers, people at the grocery store, feed store and post office. Pretty wild social life eh?

A few of us, people I had met through food stuff, started meeting weekly and began tossing ideas around of how to help local farmers and local eaters. Honestly Mom it was so freaking awesome to work with people again. They were all really interesting people and there was so much passion and enthusiasm for ideas and change when we worked together. Just the kind of people I love to be around.

We decided to work towards building a root cellar. For a few months we met weekly, brought a couple more people on board and slowly our idea began to take shape. We then heard about a local grant that could be available to us. We would have to compete with two other projects, and had only three weeks to prepare.

We all worked really, really hard and got a TON of work done Mom. We had our board of directors and had also now created sub–committees. I was going to a minimum of three meetings per week; in addition to everything I was doing on the farm. I was incredibly busy and very, very scheduled.

Our project had three moving parts – Store, Distribute, and Educate. We would build a root cellar to store veggies for farmers, create a distribution system to help get that food to people nearby and offer classes on how to cook seasonal produce.

The big day came in the blink of an eye. The other two presentations were amazing and we couldn't get a read from the judges on whose project they favoured. They deliberated over lunch.

And the envelope please...

We won!!! $125,000 now at our disposal to support our project. How kick ass was that! All of our hard work paid off. We were featured on the radio and in all the local papers. It felt so amazing knowing I was part of something that would really make a difference. I love working with people who really get stuff done.

And speaking of our community Mom, are we ever lucky to live in the one we do. Time and time again it comes together to help each other. Last year there was a terrible flood in Constance Bay. The water just kept rising and seriously threatened many homes. Everyone dropped what they were doing, not just from the Bay but from miles around and hundreds of people went to help fill sandbags and help out.

I went to help too, and at one point was moved to tears by the sense of togetherness and camaraderie Mom. We were all working side by side, helping people we didn't even know simply because it was the right thing to do. It was such an amazing experience Mom. People are awesome.

Those emails I had sent late winter were starting to pay off too. Live 88.5 – a local Ottawa radio station called me for an interview. This was the first "live" media thing I had done. I was so jittery that morning I think I had two nervous poos.

The interview went really well, although I don't think I took a breath once through the whole taping. I didn't care if I sounded nervous; at least I got my butt on the radio right?

That spring I got a call from a guy named Jean–Luc who owned a fitness studio in Ottawa. He had somehow heard about our gardening workshops and wanted to sign up a group of his staff for it. Hells yes! I sold out a whole workshop in one phone call.

A couple of days later he came with a friend to see our farm, and take some shots to add to a video he was making. How cool was that? We had a ton of fun on his visit, and he seemed to really like what we were doing. After he left, I googled him for some odd reason. Turns out he was a very accomplished, successful entrepreneur and here he was taking time out of his busy day to come and see our little slice of heaven. He started referring his clientele to us. Again, so true how a simple hello can lead to a million things. .

A couple of months later his fitness studio was having a customer appreciation night and I was invited – again – totally flattered. Everyone was dressed up and seemed so glamorous. I definitely felt like a duck out of water. I made sure to wear a pretty dress, with a lovely long scarf that would hide any sweat stains in case the pit sauce factory fired up.

I sat with a lovely woman and we began chatting about this and that, and what we both did. She was from India and taught me some great gardening tips they did back home. Soon the manager, a lovely woman began giving a speech thanking everyone for coming, and talking about their new partnerships. She began giving shout outs, wanting those people she named to put up their hands so everyone would know who they were. She said my name! Everyone looked and smiled at me, which made me feel like a million dollars.

What I remember most was the look on the lady's face that I was sitting with. She had cocked her head to the side, and was clearly now looking at me in a whole new light. Hard to describe it I guess Mom, whatever that look said, but it really meant a lot to me.

It was the same look I would get from customers when I would tell them about my education. Most people I didn't bother mentioning it to, but then there would be the odd few I felt would talk down to me. That doesn't work well for me at all. I would gently work into the conversation how I have 7 years of university and college education, and how I finished all three programs with an A+ average.

I realize school isn't everything Mom, and definitely doesn't define someone's intelligence or worthiness, but I worked my ass off to get those pieces of paper and I am damn proud of it. I know you know the feeling, I still boast how you received the Senate Medal - the highest possible award given at Carleton University. Guess we're both smarty pants.

The day finally came to pick up our first worker from Australia. Wa–freakin–hoo! I met her, and we shared the best hug, another great thing I learned from you. How to hug, I mean really hug someone, so they feel it. Hugs can say so much more than words, I learned that after you left. People wouldn't know what to say, but would say it all when they held me, not just hugged me.

Since then, I never let go first in a hug. It's neat how you can feel the instant the other person decides to really hug you back. Human contact is so important, and Mom, you'd laugh at how afraid we are of it now. Nobody is allowed to touch anybody for fear of it being 'misinterpreted'. Teachers literally aren't even allowed to pat kids on the back for a job well done. Totally ridiculous.

When the Auzzie and I got back to the Farm, I showed her around and then left her to get cozy and unpack in the trailer. I started seeding some carrots and in an instant she was right beside me, helping me seed and joking along. Her accent was so great.

It brought me right back to those few months I lived in a car touring around Australia. I still can't believe I left with only $27 in my pocket. Thank goodness my income tax rebate came in two days later, as planned.

We had a blast working together that first week. She had this habit of singing sentences instead of saying them. It was hilarious, and before long I was doing it too without even noticing.

We were setting up our planting shed again – we had to take it down every winter or the snow load would wreck it. It all started to go very wrong. It was ridiculously windy and the sides kept flapping around before I could tie them down. I was losing my mind. She kept singing a play by play of how angry I was getting.

At first my head was about to blow off, but then it got to the point I just burst out laughing. I saw, truly, how ridiculous I was being and getting all huffy over a job I just should have put down for another day. We stuck to it and got it up.

The next day we were grocery shopping and I got a text from Chris. It was a picture of our day old beautifully erected plastic shed – blown ten acres away and caught up in a fence. Arg! Gotta love farm wind.

A couple of weeks after our Auzzie arrived, she and I headed to Montreal to pick up our other worker flying in from Belgium. We would spend the day in the city and then pick her up that night. Ten minutes from the airport the van broke down. Thank goodness Lisa lived nearby and she came and rescued us, brought us to the airport and then put us all up for the night.

The next morning they got to learn all about CAA and we had a few hours to take in the city. We enjoyed poutine and somehow ended up in a part of town filming a Kevin Spacey movie. Pretty neat to see all the lights, camera and action stuff. Soon the van was fixed and we made our way back to the Farm. We all told really bad jokes the whole ride home and laughed non-stop. They were so much fun.

Always makes me laugh the first time I give our helpers their daily chore list. One of the main chores being to check out the cow's vaj–j's. The ladies also found it very amusing how they'd have to search the whole farm to find wherever the chickens decided to lay their poop fruit that morning. I was so glad to pass off that job; I didn't have time for scavenger hunts.

                                         Cheers Mom

The veggie CSA was running as smooth as butter. We were still hand watering most of the garden, and were always happy to do so. The ladies were great at everything they did. The four of us, our two helpers, Katie and I would often have lunch together on the days she'd come to pick up for deliveries. It was so awesome to be surrounded by such great women, and they loved cooking lunch for us all too – bonus!

One night we were all having a few drinky poos and I said to Chris that if he built me a proper planting shed, we could get two more rescue horses he had found. I should've known better than to open my mouth.

Four days later I had the most amazing planting shed Mom, built out of recycled everything. It had a sink, two full length counter tops running down both sides, a massive whiteboard (of course) and a huge window that could swing open. He put in that beautiful stained glass window of yours that I have been holding onto for years, the one you made for Dad's parents. It was so nice to have a piece of you nearby. It was like a warm hug every time I went to work in the morning.

The day after he finished it, a trailer came down the driveway with the new hay burners. They were really nice calm animals, on the older side. We got them through the same lady as last time, who assured me there were no "zorse" possibilities.

I had somehow landed a government contract that summer to teach two one hour workshops, back to back. They didn't have a confirmed list but said it could be upwards of 100 people. Holy cow Mom! I had done lots of presentations by this point, but always to smaller groups. Hitting the big O – Town to teach government professionals was a bit nerve racking, but again by now I was comfortable with being uncomfortable. Speaking in front of people whose outfits cost more than we spent in two weeks on groceries was a little intimidating to say the least. But I did it, and it went great. Someone even ended up signing up for the Meat CSA afterwards.

Myself, Sammy and Dana decided to do a "Mud Hero" race that July. It's a 6 km absolutely crazy obstacle course, and obviously the whole race involves mud – lots of it.

People of all shapes and sizes raced, and everyone helped each other. I remember one lady was all of four foot nothing and couldn't reach the bottom in one of the pits we had to wade across. A bunch of us formed a human chain, pulling her across until she had made it the whole way. We all cheered and clapped. People are awesome.

One day in late July the ladies and I came in for lunch from harvesting. I looked down the field and noticed one cow was lying off by herself. It looked like there was something coming out of her backside. I handed the ladies the binoculars so they could see too. I walked down the field to make sure it was a calf and not another nasty prolapsed rectum.

It was Crazy Bitch. I got about 40 feet from her, stopped and with relief saw it was two front hooves and a nose coming out of her back end. Phew.

She had been lying down and when she noticed me she lifted her head, looked right at me and gave me an "I am going to kill you" death stare. I guess she saw me and thought it was my fault she was having so much pain.

I knew right then I was in trouble, big trouble. She stood up and started to charge me. I ran like hell but she was faster than me, and I didn't make it to the fence. I tripped and hit the ground at full speed, skidding along on my face. In a flash she was on top of me, pouncing on me like a cat would on a mouse.

I remember my survival instincts kicking in. I rolled on my back; I could let her break her arms or legs but had to protect my internal organs. Holy cow Mom, I was so scared.

I could feel her hooves coming down on me, hard. I didn't even feel the pain I was so full of adrenaline. I knew she had done some damage, I could feel my clothes getting wet with blood. I remember she reared up to do another pounce and I took that split second to roll out from under her and get up and run again for the fence. I knew there was no time to roll under it so my only option was over it, and I would only have one chance. Just as I got to the fence I jumped as if on a springboard and bounced up and did a dive roll over the 5' fence. I was finally safe. Thank you Mom for driving me to gymnastics so many nights all those years ago. It saved me!

I was covered in blood, and really freaked out. I walked about 50 feet from the fence and collapsed. Nope, can't stay here. I got up and made it back to the house. I got in the kitchen and one of the ladies had 911 on the phone. I told her to hang up. They could bring me to the hospital themselves, and save the ambulance for really broken people.

I knew I was in shock, and we had to work fast. I told our Auzzie worker to quickly take off my clothes and see where all the blood was coming from; I wanted to know what we were dealing with. Thankfully we only found cuts and bruises, that weren't at all life threatening.

I had the Belgium drive, no way was this the time to teach someone how to drive on to the other side of the road. I am all for adventure but I had had enough that day. I made them stop at Fred's house to ask him to please check on Crazy Bitch. He looked at me and told me I was an idiot for caring about a cow that just tried to kill me, and to get my butt to emergency. 10–4.

We started driving to the hospital, the Belgian very focused and quite stressed. There was so much tension I had to lighten the mood. So I slumped over and pretended to have fallen unconscious. "OH NO SHE'S DEAD!" one of them screamed. I promptly popped up in my seat and started laughing. They didn't think it was funny, but I found it hilarious.

We get to the emergency room and by this time Chris has made it there too. Man was he a sight for sore eyes. I had kept a stiff upper lip until that point, but seeing him made me know I was really safe. It turned out all of my inner guts were fine, thank goodness.

I had a finger ripped open, a bad knee gash, a 3" slice down on my face, a bruised bicep that was the perfect outline of a cow's hoof and a bunch of other bruises showing up. My left calf was the worst hit.

I tried to play it cool the rest of the day and into the evening but I was pretty shaken up. By now the bruises had come out in full force, and I was black and blue. What really had me worried was the gigantic baseball that had grown out the side of my calf. I had to go back a few days later to get the stitches out from my hand and I asked about my leg. It was a hematoma – basically a humungous blood blister. It went away a few weeks later after lots and lots of slathers of an essential oil concoction I had a friend make up for me. Phew.

That night I was standing in the garden – my happy place and telling myself to get over it. The horses were in the next field and started running towards me. That sound of thundering hooves getting closer and closer brought it all back to me and I burst into tears. It was awful. I came in and had an ugly cry in Chris' arms. The physical scars are long gone, but Mom to this day I am still nervous around the cattle, and will NEVER go near a cow that's calving unless I absolutely have to and have help with me.

Later that summer the ladies and I went to Todd and Orly's annual 'cottage week' party. We are still as tight as ever, they are doing great and have two beautiful kids ours love to play with. About eight of us adults decided to play Cards against Humanity. It is not a very politically correct game, to say the least; you'd be horrified Mom. You can only play with people you know very well, or you will look like a racist, insensitive jerk.

One player reads a question or a fill in the blank sentence, and the other players have to choose the best answer from their ten possible answer cards. I remember at one point none of us could speak we were laughing so hard, and I think I peed a little. What set us off on a laugh–a–palooza was the question; "Oh, Great! It's my favourite scent, I just love breathing in _______". The winning answer was "Necrophilia". Like I said, completely inappropriate, but absolutely hilarious.

There was some funny business going on at the farm too. 'Dave the Duck' would often be playing piggyback with his three lady ducks.

One day our Auzzie helper and I walked around the pig barn to find Dave at it once again. I had told her about how a duck's penis is shaped like a corkscrew, and now she could see for herself. I guess he had just finished his business because a moment later he fell off her, his long pink man part flopping on the ground.

The female duck stood up, did the walk of shame over to the pond and started to splash around and wash the naughty off. Dave stood up, seemingly quite proud of himself, and then began projectile vomiting everywhere. I don't mean a little cough of phlegm Mom, but full on serious throwing up, hitting the barn three feet away kind of throwing up. Farm life at its best.

The ladies and I went to Kingston one weekend late summer. We went down to watch our cousin Mike play a live show. He has such an amazing voice; I used to love listening to him sing as he puttered around the apartment when we lived together. He was my favourite roommate of all time for sure, and I had a lot. We're still as tight as ever.

We went over to his bandmates place earlier for some pre-show festivities and then rode to the show in the big van with all the guys and the equipment. It was so fun, we felt like groupies. In between songs he even took the time to thank us for making the drive to come and see him, so nice. Dad and both his brothers showed up too, it was a great night with so much family together.

On the way home from Kingston somehow the conversation came around to manifesting and law of attraction stuff. I decided for fun to try to manifest something on the way home. I had had great luck last time with planters so I went with the same theme, this time going big and wanting a bathtub. It would make a nice small garden outside of their trailer.

I know it must sound crazy, that a bathtub would just magically appear for us somehow between Kingston and Ottawa, but I was getting really good at having things happen that I wanted by that point. I would just focus on being grateful for what I wanted coming into my life, and not pay any attention to worrying about the 'how'.

I kid you not Mom, not an hour into the drive we drove by a big beautiful bathtub on someone's front lawn, with a 'free' sign taped to it. Crazy eh? And let me tell you Mom, it's pretty tricky fitting a full size bathtub into the back of a Honda minivan, but we got it done.

By now I was getting really busy, and brought Darlene back for a weekly house clean. It was so great to have her around again Mom, I still remember when she lived here helping out when I was a little girl. She still cleans like nobody's business, and I was so lucky she was able to fit us in. I have cleaned this house for enough years, I am happy to pay her to do it, and love our Thursday morning coffee visits.

She is so good to the kids too Mom, always has a birthday present for them or money to go to the Carp Fair. You know how there are people from your childhood that you remember for a lifetime? Well she definitely is one for me, and I love knowing that she will be the same for our kids too.

That season was definitely the best season yet. The helpers made my life so much easier, in so many ways, in addition to the Farm work they did. Having them take over making supper during the week was a life saver, as was helping keep the kids happy and busy.

The help with the kids was such a game changer. We don't have babysitters, we never have. Having people built in to watch the kids so Chris and I could steal away, and spend time OFF the farm together was so wonderful. It gave me some sanity back.

This season it got to where I was so organized that we didn't have to work weekends any more. It was great Mom, so great. We had been working 7 days a week for three years and finally we could take a break. Such a great feeling of accomplishment. There was nothing we couldn't do.

Chapter 9

- Sadhguru

Balancing It All

We had had an amazing summer, all of us. The CSA's were going well; we really got into the swing of both of them. I was really busy though Mom and I fully realize it was me who put all those things on my plate.

I was keeping the veggie and meat CSA going, keeping two full time workers busy, going to monthly NFU meetings, at least three weekly root cellar meetings and trying to balance finding time with the kids and keeping the house going too. I thought I had it all under control by the fall of 2015, until one Saturday morning.

The kids – the KIDS called a kitchen table meeting for just the family. They were 7 and 8. They told me point blank how I loved the business more than them. I was spending too much time on the computer and with the helpers, and I was forgetting about the family. I burst into tears. I knew they were right. Here I was thinking I had it all under control, and the things that I needed to take care of most I was ignoring.

It was a blast from the past Mom. I remember, in the mid 80's Ryan and I did the exact same thing to you, in the same kitchen at the same table. I knew the instant they started talking to me exactly how they felt. I had to make a change. We had to do something as a family that got us and my head completely out of the Farm and business for a while.

We decided to go to Maine for a week. We didn't really have the money but we'd *figure it out*.

We had everything planned, and started packing. A few days before we were meant to leave Chris hurt his back, badly. He couldn't do anything and was in a hell of a lot of pain, and for him to show pain Mom, it must have been excruciating.

We got an emergency meeting with a lady who could help him, not a chiropractor, but something like it. She had him put on these funny rubber shoes, and stand in front of a vertical table, and then slowly the table tipped and became horizontal, with him on it.

She took this little tool, "the activator" which when she used it was like a quick – and safe – punch. She started working on his spine where it was out of alignment, moving it no more than 3mms with every little punch. When she first assessed him, it turned out his spine was out 2"!!! No wonder he looked like a question mark. It only took her 15 minutes to get his spine back in place. He went back two days later for his final adjustment. His pain was better and off we went to Maine.

The kids were so excited; they had never gone away anywhere before, let alone to a different country. We were so thrilled to be able to show them the ocean. We packed up a few clothes; some body boards and headed off.

We had an absolutely amazing vacation Mom. It was so wonderful to be with just the family, no helpers, no customers, no emergency animal crap, just us. The kids were great surfers and we'd play in the water for hours. Everything at home went well, thank goodness, while we were gone. We got home refreshed and I had a new set of eyes for everything. A vacation was exactly what I needed – no wonder people go on them every year.

While away, I read a couple more books about the subconscious mind and how we process thoughts and emotions. One thing that I realized was what a "lack mentality" I had in regards to anything to do with money. That was a huge lightbulb that went off Mom.

I hadn't realized it until then, but every time I thought of money it made me angry and resentful. If I felt negatively about money – there was no way I could be attracting it. I didn't want to be like that anymore.

I started to change the language I used around money, so I would feel better about it and see it as a good thing. Instead of focusing on what we couldn't afford, I would think about what we could do to make more money to afford what we wanted. I went from focusing on lack and debt to brainstorming and list making with actionable tasks. I went from reactive to proactive, so now I had the power to change the situation.

I even did a three week on-line program – paid this time – that happened to show up right then, of course. I had to pick a goal, work through the steps and make it happen. My goal became to make $2000 the following week. I followed the steps and guess what Mom – I made $2500 extra the next week! Not from anything to do with farming, but through a ton of other options I never would have thought of had I not been pushed to think outside the box. The program was worth every penny, and I have used the same principles time and time again to make extra cash when I need to.

I was so overflowing with positivity and momentum and happy thoughts that I decided to write a book, starting that fall. It would be an inspirational book helping teach people how to believe in themselves, and share everything I had learned.

I spent a lot of time throughout the winter going through all of our Facebook posts since we began, making a chronological diary of everything we had been through. I would use our story as an example of how it can all come together when you learn how to change your thinking. We were living our dream and I wanted to inspire others to go after theirs.

I know I was already ridiculously busy, but this definitely was something that quickly became very important to me Mom. It had nothing to do with farming or food, but everything to do with happiness and growth. Two things I think everyone can always use a little more of.

By mid-fall the veggie CSA was winding down – thank goodness as my body was starting to fall apart. After pumping out enough veg for twenty families for five months, my back and shoulder were absolutely killing me.

Our Belgian had gone back home but the Auzzie stayed until the end of November. One night we drove up to the store in Kinburn in freezing rain to grab some milk. On the way back she was chatting and joking, being her jolly self and I had to tell her she couldn't talk, or sing or make any noise at all. She didn't understand why driving in a little rain had my knuckles so white on the steering wheel.

I stopped, very carefully on the road just before I turned into the driveway. I told her she should get out and try walking a bit on the road. She looked at me like I had three heads. She opened the door, took one step and went ass over tea kettle. She got up and tried to take another step and down she went again. I had a good chuckle over it. Pretty sure now she understands the difference between a little sprinkle and freezing rain.

A few days later we had a dusting of snow on the ground when we woke up. She headed outside and I joined her. It was so fun Mom to see someone see snow for the first time. She jumped around like a kid at Christmas, throwing snow in the air and making happy faces on the car windows, appreciating the beauty of winter.

I was feeling way better about balancing everything by now. I was making sure to have family time, still working hard on growing the business and spending time writing the book. I made changes and things changed. Most importantly, everyone was happy.

I was contacted by the "Landowner" magazine to do an article early winter. The lady showed up just as I was feeding the cows. She herself had cattle so I didn't feel too awkward asking her to do the gates for me, and of course she was happy to. We had a great visit, her daughter showed up soon after we began chatting to take some pictures. Luckily it was a bright sunny day, and she didn't have to brave the freezing temperatures as the poor lady from the Citizen had.

I went to the post office a few weeks later for our mail and my jaw dropped while flipping through it. The magazine article had come out, and I ended up being on the cover Mom! A wonderful close-up of me, holding a chicken. Talk about humbling. Somehow to me being on the cover of a magazine solidified that I was actually "somebody". It felt amazing Mom.

One day soon after I was helping staff our NFU booth at the Ottawa Valley Farm Show. At the entrance to the show the flow of traffic took everyone right past the booth with the magazines on display, the ones with me on the cover.

When I quit the Government, Mom, there was a group of guys in the building beside me. They had always intimidated me a little, and I felt like they laughed at me when I left to become a 'farmer'. I felt as though they thought I would never be able to do it.

That same group of guys had come to the Farm show and ended up at our NFU booth, with the magazine in their hand. They seemed to look at me in a different light now. It felt really good Mom. To be honest, inside I was screaming "Ha, in your face!"

In addition to everything I had this idea for a gardening app, you know because I didn't have enough to do. An "app" Mom, is a program that you download onto your phone, some you buy and some are free, that will do calculations and figure things out for you.

There were lots of gardening apps out there, but there was always something missing from them that I had been teaching in all of my workshops. If I could create an app that incorporated it, it would really help people get the most out of their gardens. I would also have something to sell that would generate revenue without breaking my back. I had to start thinking more in these terms Mom; I realize I am not getting any younger.

So many people I had been working with, pretty much all of them, loved gardening but got so discouraged by midsummer with the weeds and bugs and plants falling over that they'd just give up. My app would make calculations for any garden dimensions: give the exact spacing, what to plant where and when, and plan for crop rotations. It would have them most likely planting the same amount in half the space they usually did, decreasing their labour and increasing their yield.

I was starting to feel the strain of everything that I had put on my plate, that was not just full now but completely overflowing. I don't know why I think I have to work so hard, why I think I have to constantly be impressing people. It's not like anyone ever says they are disappointed in me, it's just this pressure I put on myself, to keep being better.

I knew the more I learned about how to get my brain working better, everything else would fall into place. I was spending as much time on that as on the business. I was reading books, lots of books and taking on-line courses, same old thing – anything and everything I could to master my mind. The only thing was, there was just too much going on in it by midwinter to keep the balance.

Chris was now back to winter hours come January 2016, and I was trying to do as much of the farm work as I could, so when he did come home after his twelve hour work day he could actually sit down, put his feet up and enjoy the kids, who missed him terribly. I was killing myself doing it all, but not realizing it. It was Tom who started piping up and reminding me.

I wasn't eating properly and wasn't sleeping enough. My anxiety was coming back, Tom's voice getting louder and louder in my head. He is such a jerk Mom. He had been there all along, chanting his "what ifs" but I had been really good at mastering my thoughts and having nothing for him to complain about. Wherever there was the potential for disaster, I would put a system in place to alleviate it - the freezer temperature checklist for example.

This winter though, Tom started going on about things that I had no control over, the main one being that our well water would get contaminated.

That spring we were having a couple weeks of warmer and then colder temperatures, the frost coming out of the ground in bits and pieces. One morning I went to get a drink of water and it was very muddy. I guess the frost had somehow moved something in the well casing. My stomach sank. No water for the animals was one of my biggest triggers for anxiety, and we hadn't had to deal with it since the well had gone dry three years before.

We just had to wait for a day until the water settled. That day was absolute hell though Mom. Of course it was a day the van was in the shop and I had no vehicle to run and get more water, my plan being to just keep refilling big blue water jugs from friends' houses nearby and dumping them into the cow trough.

Dad was so great, as always, and offered to do whatever he could to help. He brought me some full bottles and the cows would drink it as soon as I filled it, but of course not everybody got a drink. Dad had a full day booked; no way could I ask him to help me. I started melting snow on the woodstove. Turns out it's just like maple syrup, you start out with lots and then end up with hardly anything.

Tom was having a blast, his voice screaming in my ear how all the cows would die if I didn't do better. There was still lot of snow they could eat, they would have been completely fine but that wasn't at all the way I was thinking. It was definitely a worst case scenario kind of day.

I remember I had finally melted enough to fill two bottles yet again, I was dragging them on a sled out to the cow barn, Stella ran by and somehow they both fell over, losing their make shift Saran Wrap and elastic tops, and the water poured out.

I fell to my knees Mom. The tears started to come, at full force. I was almost hyperventilating. I was so completely exhausted. I looked up at the sky and screamed in the loudest voice I could "I WON"T QUIT!" It was definitely the lowest point I had had since we started. My enthusiasm, emotions and energy were all at rock bottom.

The rest of the day I plodded through, I had no other choice. Of course all the animals were just fine, the water settled down and we could drink it again by the next morning.

The next week I had the water tested. Tom had convinced me there would be e-coli in it and he was right, it had 1 e-coli per 100 parts per million. It was the smallest possible number it could be, but it made me so sick to my stomach I almost threw up. We treated the well, tested it again and it was fine. Tom though, being the jerk that he was, had convinced me that it could change again at any moment. I listened to him and felt anxious every second from that moment on.

It was so ridiculous Mom, I had done so much studying, researching and learning all about the mind and how whatever you think about, good or bad, you bring into your life. No matter how much I tried not to think about it, I kept focusing on the fact that the water could somehow get e-coli again. Over the next season I had it checked no less than 5 times, and every single time it was totally fine. It didn't shut him up one bit though.

The other thing that Tom kept me paranoid about was that somehow before we got the fence up that a farm animal would get out and into the garden, contaminating it with its poopy feet. It got so bad I would check gates and latches 10 times a day Mom, no word of a lie. I felt like I was slowly going mad. It was horrible.

One day soon after I went outside and there was a pig standing on the front lawn, he saw me and bolted right to the garden. Arg! He only walked down the very back of it, and...then right into the barn where I closed him in, thankfully. I had not closed the gate properly the night before when I was doing my OCD open and close routine. No matter how many times I saw it close, I would walk back to the house and go back and do it again. I guess on my last time I told myself to hurry up and that I was being ridiculous, and that is when I hadn't latched it fully.

My anxiety was worse that day than it ever had been, including the muddy water day. One of my worst fears, one that I couldn't stop focusing on had come true. The thing was, looking back, it really couldn't have gone better. Nothing was seeded or planted, it was still early spring and he walked along the back so I could just switch up the planting scheme so nothing would ever be planted there. But of course that wasn't good enough for Tom, even with all I did to ensure no food went where the pig had.

I could clearly see where the pig had walked. It hadn't rained in a while so the soil was as dry and crusty as could be. It was easy to see his faint footprints, so I dug out the soil around them – a 2" x 2" footprint and I would dig a foot of soil around it – total overkill, but I had to do everything I could to shut him up. Still no dice though, Tom kept nagging me that it could happen again.

Chris had noticed that I hadn't been myself in days. He kept asking me what was wrong but I wouldn't open up. I was so embarrassed that I was worrying so much about something that had been done and dealt with.

Then finally I told him, everything that was worrying me, my constant nausea and overwhelming anxiety. He was so great Mom, I mean really great. He would go over it with me, gently reminding me how I done exactly what I needed to get rid of the problem. The well and the garden would be fine. Nobody would die from eating our food. I felt better, but was nowhere near 100%. Tom was still there, his constant murmurs keeping me on edge.

I decided to just sink myself into work even further, and keep my mind busy on what I wanted it to be busy with. I worked tirelessly on the app, the book, improving the workshops and the website. With spring just around the corner, I had to find new helpers too.

We ended up hiring another girl from Belgium who would be here a couple of months, and one from England who would join her halfway through and then stay on longer. A German girl would arrive soon after the first girl left, so we'd always have two people here full time for the height of the vegetable season.

I was definitely happy to be welcoming new faces and new life to the farm soon. I was so disappointed in myself Mom for letting Tom take such a front seat the last part of winter, and worrying so much about things that weren't really that big a deal. I forgave myself and moved on. The snow was going and good times were ahead. That is what I focused on.

Chapter 10

"Just underneath your breaking point lies your true strength."

- Jennifer Tindugan-Adoviso

Losing My Mind

So Mom, before I go onto the hell that was the spring and summer of 2016 please, please know that I am alright now. I am not going to embellish or exaggerate at all this next part of the story; this is actually what I went through. Again though Mom, know that I have worked through all the crap, and it's some pretty heavy crap, and I am much, much better now.

It seemed we were all set up for the upcoming season as we had been for the last season – both our veggie and meat CSA's sold out. I had heard from many people, and even the Farmers' Almanac was calling for a really hot, dry year. The possibility of running out of water definitely had my anxiety on high, and Tom was loving it. I was so overworked with all of the meetings and computer, farm and house work that I had taken on. I just didn't have the energy to keep finding the rainbow, and I couldn't shut him up.

He would say if we ran out, all the veggies would instantaneously die, as would the animals and our business. So I did what I always did when my anxiety was getting worse – I planned ahead. When I picked up our first worker in Montreal I also picked up two huge 1000L water totes. We filled them up straight away when we got home. The well was high at that time but I knew it wouldn't be for long. It didn't shut him up completely, but at least quieted him for a bit.

Our second worker arrived soon after our first and quickly got the hang of seeding and weeding, thankfully. Working in the garden definitely had a different feel then it had the year before though Mom, there wasn't the same fun and laughter. My growing anxiety over the impending water crisis or possible contamination had me on edge, my black cloud affecting everybody's day.

I had sent in a water test yet again to check its quality before we started putting any on the garden. It came back inconclusive, they couldn't' test it because apparently it was unsightly. Tom started doing the two step. I filled a cup and realized that there were really, really tiny little red balls in it. After a while on the computer I found out what it was. Turns out when your water softener breaks, a gazillion of these little beads are released in the water – totally harmless, but this was why the lab had rejected our sample. Arg!

At the same time, the peas were coming up in the garden, the first thing we had seeded. They needed a drink but I wasn't comfortable using our water until I had back positive test results from the next sample I sent in. Of course we were drinking it and totally fine but it is a whole different ball of wax when you are selling commercially. I bought some big blue Culligan bottles of water and would pour it into juice containers and water the peas that way.

I knew I was being completely ridiculous and irrational. I had gotten perfect water test results a couple of weeks before, and nothing had changed so surely the water would be fine. But again, Tom's worst case scenario song was on full blast in my head, so I just decided not to risk it. I had done a lot of research about the lifespan of e-coli and knew if for any reason it got in the garden, it would be there for months. No way was I going to do anything that would make that even remotely a possibility.

The next water test came back perfectly fine – of course. By now it was a couple of weeks since we had filled the totes, and watering the garden now had the well very low. I had emptied the first tote with it still on the ground, and the lower its' water level, the slower the water came out. A real pain in the butt and very time consuming. So I decided to put the second full tote on a wagon to speed up the water pressure. When I lifted it, the tractor almost tipped forward and I almost pooped my pants Mom. I had no idea how heavy water was. Mental note – fill totes ON the wagon in the future.

Once the second tote was empty, I tied them both down to the wagon and brought them to Katie's' place to refill – about ten minutes away. Her water had tested fine and she had a kick ass well, I could take as much as I needed whenever I needed it. I didn't care if it took a few hours a week to get it, it was clean and safe and unlimited.

Katie had seen a wee taste of my anxiety the year before but now saw the real extent of it. I couldn't tell the helpers what was really going on in my head; it wasn't their business or their problem. Katie was my leaning post; she always made time to gently walk me through my worries and always made me feel better. She was so amazing to work with. I never, ever would have made it through that year without her being who she is, as a business partner and friend.

With both totes now full from her place, I started to head home. The trailer started to weave on the road with so much momentum from the water sloshing around. My leg was shaking like a leaf on the pedals, and my stomach was turning. My anxiety went through the roof, I wanted to be sick. I got the wagon back under control and crawled at a snail's pace and finally made it home. I vowed never to do it again. It just wasn't safe. I'd have to figure something else out. Damn.

There were some pretty cool things going on at that time too Mom, reminding me that the real world was out there, waiting for me.

In May I was invited to speak at an elementary school. I was teaching pretty much the whole school by individual classes, there were about 8 of them. I was so nervous. Not at all about what I'd say, but that I would bring something in that would get on someone's food and they'd die. I washed my hands four times between when I got to the school and when I started teaching.

You know its funny Mom, I remembered years and years ago watching a show about anxiety and OCD, before I had any idea what it was really about. It was about a woman who spent 10 hours a day with her rituals of making sure the stove was off, the door closed and that things were in their place. For an exercise, a psychologist moved one of her sons' dinosaurs from its bin into the bin for cars.

She started to sweat and rock back and forth. You could physically see how much she was struggling. I couldn't understand it, it was just a toy. I realized that day at the school, washing my hands countless times, that I had become her. It was quite the moment Mom. I talked myself out of the panic attack I could feel coming, was compassionate with myself, and regained control.

Of course the talks went fine; actually the whole day was quite enjoyable. I had forgotten how hard it is to keep the attention of really little people for more than two minutes. The kindergardeners and younger grades were really squirmy and sat there picking their noses and interrupting me to tell me about their grandmothers' tomatoes or how they helped plant sunflower seeds. Super cute. The older ones didn't seem really interested either; they were way too busy trying to look for each other. Two hours of teaching paid for our groceries that week.

That spring I was also invited to participate in an exposition on health and wellness in Ottawa. I was a little bit nervous to be at such a big venue, they were expecting over 10,000 people but of course I rocked it. Anything to do with talking to people I am really good at, just like you. It is amazing how a warm smile draws a crowd so much easier than the fanciest display.

I didn't stop talking from open to close both days of the weekend. What made me feel so amazing was the number of people who would stop by our booth, and say that they followed us on Facebook and how I always made them laugh and they really loved what we were doing. Compliments like that always make everything worthwhile, and knowing that we were making people smile every day, that was such a great feeling. That is how you get remembered. After the expo I got a bunch more farm gate orders too.

The drought was in full swing by late spring. We had been being conservative with the water, but now had to be even more careful with it. We'd swim in the pool instead of showering and I'd make one dish meals as often as possible to save on washing dishes. The water shortage affected every area of our lives; it was such an inconvenience to say the least. You don't realize how much you take it for granted until you can't. I know you know what I mean.

They were calling for a storm one night, and I couldn't have been happier. FINALLY a rain, the crops and garden would get a drink as would the pastures, which had burnt to a crisp. The sky was black and the winds were picking up as we went to sleep. Tom had finally shut up, knowing the well would once again be replenished. I was more relaxed that night than I had been in weeks.

We woke up and I looked outside – nothing. The ground was still as dry as the Sahara desert – the rain had missed us. A few minutes after I came downstairs that same morning I got a call from Fred. He told me I best go look outside at the Farm, on the Carp side and that there was a lot of smoke. Huh?

I hopped in the mini-van, and drove across the hay field to see where it was coming from. I noticed some embers in the underbrush of the tree line and realized that though we didn't get any rain, lightning must have struck during the night. When I first saw them I thought I could easily stamp them out, until I noticed the embers ran for a few hundred feet. Crap. I needed help, fast.

I flew to the house and called 9-1-1. Soon after two huge fire trucks came, along with a couple of pick-ups and ATV's. It took about an hour for them to get all of the fire out. And you know the most ironic part of the whole ordeal Mom? Now there was more water than I could ever need on the farm inside those fire trucks, but no way could I ask them to spray the garden as it was from the Carp River and full of nasty stuff. Grr.

As the firefighters were leaving, I noticed a cow was off by herself in the field. Well, at least we would have the wonder of a new baby calf that morning to brighten the day. She walked around for a while and then laid down. Out came the calf shortly after, phew, we didn't have to help her at all. A few minutes later it still hadn't stood up so I went down the field to check on the baby, on the safety of the four wheeler. It was dead. And it wasn't even 9 in the morning yet.

The next while I was pretty quiet and the helpers could see how discouraged I was. At least the Mama cow was doing alright. Soon she had something else coming out of her back end. I just assumed it was the placenta.

A little while later it was still there. Fred was cutting hay for us luckily in the next field and I waved at him to come over. I asked how long should it take for it to drop out of her. We went over to the cow so he could have a better look. Fred knew right away, it wasn't the placenta, it was another calf. She didn't try to walk away at all; she knew she needed help.

I got one of our helpers to run and grab some binder twine. Fred did his MacGyver thing and looped the twine inside the Mama, around the hooves of the calf. We started pulling, as hard as we could. Let me tell you Mom it is no easy feat. A couple of minutes later and the calf came out. It was dead. There was nothing we could do. By now it was 10:30 a.m. and I had already had to deal with a fire and two dead calves. Arg!

I wanted to crawl into bed and cry myself to sleep, but I couldn't. That day we had to harvest for the veggie CSA, so I had to keep going. I was running very low in the rainbow and lollipops department for sure.

That day was definitely a changing point for me. My anxiety started to balloon out of control. It was so silly Mom, now it wasn't just about water, the garden or handling meat, is was for anything related to food.

I soon, very quietly, became obsessed with disinfecting everything in the house – sinks, taps, door handles, countertops, everything. Only problem was, dollars to doughnuts, as soon as I did a dog would freak out, a cat would jump on the counter and Tom would convince me that the cat had just walked in chicken poo or something, and now it was all over my kitchen. I'd throw all animals outside, redo my routine and almost feel normal again. Then someone would let the animals in and it would all start again. Good times.

Making lunches became a nightmare. So now Mom, with all the nut allergies you can't send your kids with anything with nuts to school. Fair enough, but now companies are covering their butts and adding "May contain nuts" to everything. With my OCD where it was now, reading ingredient labels once wasn't enough; I had to read them three and four times. And even then, I would be anxious the whole day that I had missed something and sent the boys with something that was going to kill someone. Totally ridiculous, looking back now.

Were there bacteria left on the counter that I hadn't cleaned well enough? Were there bacteria from washing our hands after chores left in the sink that would somehow get on the food I was washing before making dinner? Were the dishtowels I was using to wash my hands somehow not clean? It was like no matter what I did, no matter what systems I put in place, there was still somehow a possibility of bacteria getting on our family food.

I felt like I was slowly starting to lose it Mom; it was not a nice feeling. I was so worried all the time that even when I would go to bed, I would drift off to sleep imagining every possible negative thing that "could" happen. Then all night I would dream about catastrophes and wake up in a panic. It was a vicious circle because I would be so anxious in the morning that I couldn't eat, and then my anxiety would just keep growing through the day because I was so weak.

I definitely have a huge space in my heart now for those suffering from mental illness. Before all this crap happened to me, I admit I judged people who said they were struggling, assuming it couldn't really be that bad. But now I got it. Hurting inside feels 100x worse because no one can see it.

It was like I just couldn't be happy and just accept what was. I had to keep looking for things to be anxious about. I would actually hear myself saying "What do I need to be worrying about right now?" Seriously, how totally messed up is that???

The kids were so awesome Mom; they seemed to know just what I needed. I kept finding sticky notes they had left for me – everywhere, in my room, on my vision board and in my office. Their notes would say things like "You can do anything Mom", "You are doing amazing Mom, keep going" and inspirational things like that.

Those notes made all the difference Mom. They had learned to be positive and supportive no matter what, which made me feel like I was doing my job, which felt great. Chris was incredible. He was doing everything he could to help out with whatever he could, and never once made me feel bad about it. I picked a good one for sure.

The best part of my day would be watching the cows get silly and run around at dusk. No matter how anxious I was, watching them play tag with each other and Stella, a beautiful sunset in the background, the cool spring breeze – it always made me feel better. It was my happy place.

You know how great the sunsets can be here Mom, pink and purples covering the entire sky like a blanket. They always remind me to breathe and enjoy the here and now. I made a point to walk out to the field every night, and drink in as much of it as I could, for as long as I could. Nature is the best medicine.

I knew I had to get more pro-active about my anxiety before it got any worse. At first I started reading all about it, but then soon realized it wasn't helping – it was just creating more, so I switched gears.

I started focusing on bringing more positive things into my life that would help me. I put an app on my phone so with the touch of a button I could listen to calming sounds and follow a slowed breathing pattern, which always quieted Tom down a little. I made my phone screen savers inspirational messages, going back to the whole power of language thing.

I stopped watching mindless T.V., and stopped watching the news, way too depressing. If I listened to the radio, it would have to be stories about how people were being kind to each other, or doing good things. Even little things like if I was talking to a friend and they started drowning me in their sorrows, I would change the subject to something uplifting.

I had absolutely no time for anything that would bring me down, I was so conscious of everything I was letting in and listening to. The more and more positive I made my bubble, the easier it was to keep my mind in a good place. This is when I had to make some hard choices, and let some people in my life go, but I had to take care of me, that was the most important thing. I needed me, so I could be all I could be for them – Chris and the kids.

I started making a point to follow and pay attention on social media to people that I knew would lift me up. People like Jean-Luc, who didn't just talk about being an entrepreneur, but about all things about life, always in a positive way. I am sure to this day he has no idea how much he inspired me and kept me going when I really needed it, but wow Mom, paying attention to his words, along with others that inspired me that summer made all the difference.

One thing I did, that made a huge change in my thinking was I became diligent about writing every night in my gratitude journal, 5 things I was grateful for that happened in the day. I would do it right before I fell asleep. It kept me focused on all the good there was in my life, and that is exactly what I needed to go to sleep thinking about, the 'what is' and not 'what ifs'. There were so many great things happening every day to me, recognizing them and writing them down really helped me be present. Anxiety is all about the future, and guilt and regret are all about the past. I wanted none of any of it.

For example, one day I was fretting about all our money going to water, and I found $200 I had stashed away and forgotten about.

Or the afternoon that summer when I was dreading making supper. An old friend called me out of the blue wanting to take me out to dinner, for no special reason.

Or how one weekend last month when I didn't think I had the energy for the kids, someone called and asked to take them both for a sleepover.

It is so true Mom what you always said - there is so much good all around, you just have to stop and take a second to recognize it. It's funny how life always gives you just what you need, when you need it.

It was so nice to go back every few days and reread my gratitude journal, of all of the great things that were happening for me. It definitely always brought me back to the happy land of "what is".

Even with all the work I was doing to see the good that summer, in the back of my mind I still couldn't shut Tom up Mom. Try as I did, I couldn't ignore him, and was still giving energy to what bad things 'could' happen, and of course one did. Law of attraction, you get what you focus on, either bad or good. So glad I have since been able to train my brain to focus on the good.

That summer Chris went out to do chores one morning and found a dead calf in the field. The heat stress caused by the heat wave that came with the drought had sent the cow into labour weeks early. Now we had one

                                              Cheers Mom

calf instead of four, throwing off our breeding schedule yet again. At least we had one healthy calf right? And she was a beauty Mom, eyelashes that made me jealous.

By midsummer the well ran dry, and we had to bring in a water tanker. I ordered the biggest one I could. I was so glad that finally we didn't have to worry about it anymore, or at least for a while. We filled the totes – we had three by then, filled the pool and the well, and any extra just went on the grass around the well. It would eventually filter down through the ground and end up in the well.

I did laundry, washed the whole house, we all showered, and it was heaven. A few short days later, the well was very low again. Turns out the water had just gone out the bottom of the well as the water table was so low. ARG! We ordered another water truck, now the total was up to $500.

At the same time, the three automatic cow waterers kept leaking out of their overflow. We couldn't figure it out. We kept adjusting the float – the lever that says the water level is high enough so it should stop filling but it wasn't working properly. Turns out all of the miniscule red beads that had been let go when the water softener broke had now made their way all the way through the water lines and were clogging the floats. It kept thinking it wasn't filled up enough and would keep filling and the overflow would continuously slowly seep out the back.

The only way to get the beads gone would be to completely blow out the system, which meant turning on all of the lines running out of the well and run them at full speed, blasting out the beads. This of course would have meant emptying the well in about an hour, not an option. They weren't leaking a lot at all, but regardless, they leaked constantly.

As frustrating as all these things were Mom, there was lots of wonderful things going on too, there was always good happening for me.

A brand new customer came to the Farm one hot summer day and noticed the kids playing ball. After some chit chat he asked if perhaps he could pitch a few balls. Twenty minutes later we are all playing a full on baseball game. Four rug rats, me and a very well dressed business man in fancy shoes.

I delivered to our CSA customers in July, enjoying the quick chats we have catching up on the last month. I thought everyone had left when I heard a knock at my window. A lady was waiting for the crowd to go so she could give me the most amazing hug. Not a quick embrace with the standard double back pat, but a long, warm and wonderful hug to thank me for doing what we do. How wonderful is that!

A customer and fellow Mom stopped by the next week to buy some beef bones. I was telling her about how hard we had been working to keep the farm going with the drought. She laughed at how our most exciting meal lately had been grilled cheese and pickles. Two days later she pops by with two frozen yoghurt containers of homemade beef broth for us.

I am so truly blessed to have met the people we have, and have the customers we do, who often become friends. It makes me feel so good when they tell us how thankful they are that we do what we do, so they can eat meats that had a happy healthy life. There was one Mom who told me after a year and a half of being in our Meat CSA program, that her three kids hadn't been sick once in the past 12 months. She attributed it 100% to what they were eating - the meat and veggies coming from our farm. It absolutely made my day.

I have seen people go through so many things in their lives – weddings, divorces, having babies, even people struggling with depression. One of my favourite long-time customers stopped by for her meats and I could tell she needed a hug. I didn't ask, I just hugged her, really hugged her and her tears started flowing. I held her and wouldn't let go. She let it all out. I could see how much better she felt afterwards. How lucky was I to be able to do that for someone?

Those were the times that I was reminded what life is really all about, helping other people. Time and time again, as soon as I was 100% in that frame of mind, no anxiety keeping me living in my own bubble, only thinking of others and what I could do to give more, more and more things would show up for me to be grateful for.

The most wonderful thing happened that summer for me Mom. I was asked to give a talk on Women in Farming. My trusty tattered ol' school gas station map book led me to the address. I turned in the driveway, looked up at the building and smiled ear to ear. I was once again where I began.

It was held at your old one room schoolhouse!!! It was like the biggest, warmest, and let me assure you the most welcome hug I could have gotten from you. It came at just the right time that summer, when I needed you most.

It instantly brought back so many warm memories of all the good times growing up there riding horses, climbing in the orchard and enjoying your Mom's apple pies. They were so tasty. I dare say I make a pretty mean one myself. It's my standard Valentine's Day and Anniversary present for Chris. So true – "The fastest way to a man's heart is through his stomach."

Chatting with one of the Mom's after the schoolhouse talk, she mentioned how in her yard close by, one of the trees still stood from the original farmstead – the family's name began with an "F?" Fentiman – that was us! I couldn't believe it. It was such a wonderful thing to hear Mom, I definitely felt you all around me right then, it felt so good.

I left for home with a warm heart and while stopped at a stop light I glanced to the left and my jaw dropped again when I noticed a sign in a big garden – it read "Fentiman Park". I thought all traces of your parents and their farm were long gone and here in one night I had seen two. It was such perfect timing Mom, it let me know somehow that I would be alright.

We were breaking a record for days without rain that summer which soon would change. There was supposedly a huge storm that was coming (again) that would bring a ton of rain, refill the well and give the garden a proper drink – finally.

The storm came, and it was a doozy. Only thing was we didn't get a drop of rain Mom, instead Mother Nature delivered us another treat. A huge lightning bolt hit our hydro transformer and blew it up!!! My absolute worst fears all coming true at once – no power meant no water pumps to get the animals water, and all the freezers were now off. It blew up all of our electric fencers and TV stuff in the house. For fuck sakes! Thank goodness for the generator.

I phoned Hydro and they said they would come as soon as they could; they had a long list of poles down. I lost my mind, explained the situation and shortly after that they showed up and fixed the problem. Tom was screaming in my ear, shouting how everything I ever worried about was happening. I was so close to a total nervous breakdown but that just wasn't an option. I had to keep it together, too much and too many were depending on me. I had no other choice.

I kept working hard to stay positive. I'd read more and more books about the psychology behind believing in yourself and creating better thinking patterns. My favourite one from that time was "Think and Grow Rich" by Napoleon Hill. It had nothing to do with money, but everything to do with a positive mindset.

I also started watching all kinds of YouTube videos, again about universal energy and the law of attraction. The concepts got pretty deep sometimes, peeling back the onion layers as much as possible. It was exactly what I needed to focus on, things that I could do actively instead of focusing on what I couldn't control. Being proactive, not reactive.

Our well almost went dry yet again and we ordered another truck. Only two of the three water totes fit on the wagon at once, so there would always be at least one full one on the ground I'd have to lift onto the wagon, and go through the stress of possibly tipping yet again.

One time when I went to lift one on, I forgot I had moved the fork prongs to off centre to do another job, and hadn't moved them back. I was lifting the heavier than hell tote and all of a sudden, the tractor started to flip sideways. I slammed the forks lever forward to let the tote down as fast as I could. It landed hard on the corner of another tote, denting the metal cage around it. I couldn't move, I couldn't take my shaking leg off the brake. Not fun.

Chris got home a minute or two later, I went to him and had a total freak out Mom. All the water crap and stress and anxiety flowed out of me like a volcano. He held me for a long time as it poured out. Thank goodness the kids weren't around, I scared myself at how badly I was losing it, but I had to keep it together. I wouldn't let it beat me.

By now I had hired someone to take over our social media accounts full time. She was great, carefully following the three areas I wanted her to post about – our farm, agriculture and positivity. To the outside world it looked like we were doing amazing, and we were – I was bringing in more money than I ever had. I felt like such a total phony though. Nobody knew the hell I was going through. They would visit the Farm and compliment us on all we had accomplished and rave about how they loved seeing all of our posts. I would smile and thank them, careful to not give away what I was really feeling. I was so full of shit it made me sick.

I had to put the idea of the book by the wayside. I knew I would get back to it, but no way could I work on it that year. There wasn't an inspired bone in my body; I was just in survival mode. I definitely missed working on it, and knew my worry wouldn't last forever and I'd get back to it someday.

By late summer I had made it a habit of leaving the farm when a water truck would come. I just couldn't mentally handle anything about water anymore; Tom would get so loud I couldn't think. I trusted our helpers, the first one had left by that point and the third had been around a few weeks. Both knew a bit about my worries and I felt comfortable leaving it all in their hands.

I started to bring things into the business too that would take me away from the farm. I began doing on-site consultations for people wanting to start a hobby farm and I'd feed off their eagerness. It got me off the farm, I was helping someone and making money.

A definite turning point for me happened late that fall. I was heading to Dad's in the minivan, which was very much on its last legs. In the past week something went in the transmission and it wouldn't go out of first gear so it was pretty much parked while we looked for another vehicle. The brakes were done too and sounded like nails on a chalkboard, but just going to the next road was fine. I was driving with a laundry basket full of dishes. Driving somewhere to do dishes, that's how bad the water situation was Mom. Totally ridiculous.

I remember driving at about 20 kms an hour and the engine was screaming. I was crying so hard I could barely see so I tried to stop and the brakes slowly screeched to a halt. I screamed at the top of my lungs "Who lives like this???" Thank goodness no other cars came as I sat there for a good five minutes in the middle of the road bawling like a baby.

I was tired, so bloody tired of stuff going wrong Mom. I was doing my best and I felt the universe just kept throwing more crap at me. Everything seemed like a test. I knew I would never give up, and I was getting pretty darn tired of proving it. And just for fun, when I went back to get the dishes later, I had forgotten to put in soap and they were still filthy. At least they got a good rinse right?

That night I decided something had to change. I had to stop telling myself the same sad story about how crappy our summer was. I had to stop putting all of my energy into it; I needed to put it into something positive. I began thinking how great it would be when we got our new vehicle. It would be just the car we wanted, and it would land right in our laps. That is what I focused on, and worked to feel that gratitude with every cell in my body, just like with the planters.

That very week Mom, a friend stopped by and told us about a dealership in Ottawa that had incredible deals on cars. We went by the next day and low and behold there was the exact car we wanted, and the cost was 50% lower than anywhere else we had seen it! It was a Ford FOCUS – the name made me smile. Everything was falling into place simply because I had changed my focus. I think a lot of people assume with manifesting and positive thinking things come to you with no effort, and they do sometimes, but you have to work for it too - like we did going to the dealership. You have to be in the right space to let things happen.

We bought the car on the spot. When I saw our new licence plates, I had to smile again. The letters were my full initials, and the numbers were my favourite numbers.

I had been meaning to go by the dealership that same week and pick up the spare key but I hadn't had the chance. A couple of days later Katie said she had to make a pit stop on the way to an NFU meeting, and drove right to the exact same dealership for her errand! Crazy eh? Good ol' law of attraction.

All in all from a business standpoint, that season was a total success. From a personal standpoint, it was a total disaster. The saving grace came late in the season with the whole car thing, reminding me that when I worked to not worry, and just trust that good things were coming my way, they came.

I knew I just had to keep going, keep working on changing my thinking and above all keep believing in myself. I can't stress again how wonderful Chris and the kids were with me throughout that season Mom. They could see in my eyes when I just needed a hug and I could feel the stress leaving my body when they held me. I wouldn't have made it without them. Family really is everything.

Chapter 11

"If you're brave enough to say goodbye,

life will reward you with a new hello."

- Paulo Coelho

Letting It Go

Normally by the time the fall came I was getting more relaxed, but not this year with the drought. I knew I was dancing on the border of crazy town with my thoughts, but also knew I just had to keep going, it wouldn't last forever.

You know how Moms have this special way of always knowing how to fix everything? You can go to them with any problem, and even if they don't know what to say, they can give you one look or a hug and instantly you feel better. Well I didn't have that, but I WAS that to everyone and everything. The responsibility of everything I had created was choking me. I had nowhere to go for that person to save me. I missed you so much, but even though I couldn't see you, I knew you were always around me. The schoolhouse talk reminded me of that.

The day I came home from the hospital, the day you left us, everything was so surreal. I walked out on the deck and sat down. Right then two blue jays – not one but two landed on the railing. They both looked at me at the same time and held my gaze. A warm hug came over me, like you were there telling me I would be okay. Since then birds have always reminded me of you, nearby but never within grasp.

One night that fall I was having a pity party by myself in the garage. I had been consumed with terrible, debilitating anxiety for two days. I was beating myself up for being such a mess. I felt like a terrible Mother because I had been so short with the kids lately. I felt guilty for all the extra work Chris was doing because I could barely function. I was in a really, really low place Mom, it was horrible.

All of a sudden a bird came from out of nowhere and hovered about a foot from my head. I spoke to it, "I know Mom, and I have to change something. I can't keep going like this. But I just can't, I'm not strong enough..." The bird, who had kept eye contact with me the whole time I spoke, bee-lined into my forehead at top speed.

I will never forget that moment. I realized you were right there and you knew you had to smack some sense into me. I knew in that instant that I was strong enough. I knew I could make a change. Thank you for that. I needed you most right then, and you found a way to show me you were there. Love you to pieces Mom.

Knowing we were heading to the beach that fall for a family vacation was my saving grace too. The only problem was the four – yes FOUR water tankers we had to order inside of 8 weeks had completely drained our savings. No way in hell we weren't going away, so I decided to write a post asking for some help. And that's a big deal for me, asking for help, admitting I didn't have it all under control.

I had been mentioning on social media how hard the drought had been for farmers, trying to keep it light but still getting the point across. My post alluded to our biggest hurdles that year and politely asked if anyone wanted to make an order for our last delivery date before we left. I put up a picture of our family, which was extremely rare; I had only shared a handful of pics of the kids over the last few years. I must have struck a chord because the orders started coming in.

And when I say coming in Mom, I mean they were pouring in one after the other. I had my email notification set to a duck quacking, so it wouldn't spook the cattle if I was working around them. That morning it sounded like there was a fully stocked pond in my pocket.

It hit me so deep Mom. It wasn't the fact that I was getting sales, it was the fact that people were offering to help. I had felt so alone in my struggle, living my secret hell every day and here I had reached out and it was clear people were listening, and wanted to help.

I remember at one point I had to pull over on a Queensway ramp because I broke down crying. I was so deeply touched by the outpouring of help for us; I can't even put it into words Mom. People are so awesome.

Our vacation that year was a life saver. We went to Maine again, and rented the same cottage as we had the year before. I hardly worked at all, only read one book and spent most all of the time with the kids and Chris. No worries, just hugs, smiles and laughter. Just what I needed.

The best thing was knowing that I had left the Farm with two very capable workers, who would handle everything perfectly. I even got them to weigh out a couple of months of meat shares when I was gone, which was huge for me – letting someone take care of what I had been obsessing about micro-managing.

One day when we were away we went to do groceries. I picked up some eggs at the grocery store, and was telling the cashier how I hadn't bought them in the last six years as we raised our own chickens. Just as I was lifting it out of the cart, the carton slipped and all of the eggs crashed and broke. You just have to laugh sometimes eh?

I was lucky enough that fall to be sent to Saskatoon for a National Farmers Convention. I love going to them Mom, sitting with such intelligent, down to earth interesting people, I always learn a lot. The trip there was uneventful, and the trip home I assumed would be the same. Not so much.

I had a layover, can't remember where and right before boarding they announced the flight had been pushed back another hour. Everyone waiting to go got really cranky. The whole feeling in the lounge changed. It was totally ridiculous Mom, it was only an hour. I decided to change that feeling, for everyone.

Again, this goes back to the whole 'I honestly don't care if I look ridiculous if I can make people smile' idea. I stood myself in the middle of the lounge, in front of all the seats and started to dance. At first it was just a little bit, and then a couple of minutes later I was pulling out my best disco moves. Everybody was now smiling and had forgotten about the delay. I had brightened everyone's day.

When we started boarding, I got up to show them my passport and pass and felt a tap on my shoulder. It was the captain. He had seen the whole boogie deal, and said he wanted to repay me for keeping all the passengers happy while they waited. He invited me up to the cockpit during boarding. HOW COOL WAS THAT!! Just goes to show Mom, what goes around comes around, always.

Another fun time I had that fall was at Wymkin. It's an annual party I started having back in 2012 for my birthday. It stands for "Women in Kinburn", and there is a strict no kids or males rule. It's a pot luck where usually no less than 10 ladies and I would get together, fill and I mean FILL the kitchen table with food and drink, stuff our faces and laugh until the early hours of the morning. The room would be filled with my oldest friends, often the only time I saw them was at the party. It was always so nice to be with friends who didn't want anything from me but my company.

I have learned that to be a good friend Mom is knowing when to shut up. People sometimes just need to get stuff off their chest and need someone to tell it to. They don't want someone to 'fix' them or solve their problems; they just need get something out. I always try to remember, we were given one mouth and two ears for a reason.

Another thing I have recognized is how so many people really don't know how to listen. Instead of really hearing you, they are just waiting for you to finish your sentence so they can say what they want to. People who start all of their sentences with "I", bringing the conversation constantly back to them. That drives me nuts. I make a real point Mom, when talking to someone, to hear what they are saying and be interested in it. I wait to speak, letting what they have just said really sink in. It's incredible what you can learn about people, when you take the time to listen.

One thing I was slowly starting to do this fall was to talk about my anxiety, with people other than Chris. I was so blown away Mom, by just how many struggle with it too. It would feel so good, knowing that I wasn't alone, I wasn't a freak, and that there were people I could talk to about it, who really knew what it was like.

The thing I realized is, everybody has shit. Nobody has a perfect life. You have no right to judge anyone, because you don't know where they are coming from, you don't know their shit. Everyone is going through something you don't know about.

There was a thing floating around a couple of years back on Facebook that always stuck with me. It said something like "Don't envy the rich kid who seems to have everything, when all they really might want is their parent's attention. Don't judge the person who seems shy and withdrawn, they might come from a broken home." It went on with a bunch more examples, all proving we have no right to judge a book by its cover. So true.

I realized when I started opening up about my anxiety, it's all about surrounding yourself with good people. That is exactly what I did to help me get through my hard times Mom. The nicest part was I didn't have to look far, and realized just how many great people I have in my life. As much work as I did myself to get better, it was those around me that really carried me through.

I think that is why I work hard to always brighten someone else's day. They might be smiling, but falling apart on the inside. Hence the importance I put on having at least a third of our social media posts be about positivity and believing in yourself. Sometimes it just takes one thing to change someone's mood in a day, which affects everything that follows – like the stubbed toe example. I wanted to do all I could to be that person.

It was so amazing Mom all the times I would meet people, or they would approach me when I was out. They would tell me how they love my positivity, and that it has made a real difference in their day.

And it is so easy, so, so easy to make a difference.

I'd do things like when holding a door open for someone, I'd make sure to catch their eye and then give them a huge smile and a cheery "You're welcome".

Or when I'd see a Mom about to lose her mind, on the way by I would pat her on the arm and tell her what a great job she was doing.

Or if someone couldn't reach something in the grocery store, I'll zoom up, grab it for them, shoot them a huge smile and then walk away, needing nothing in return.

It's so easy to show people that you notice them, and that they are important. After all, I think that is the core of what we all want. One thing I have always done too Mom is to make time for people. Of course, family always comes first.

I am so glad you raised us with such strong values surrounding family. We are as close as ever – the extended family I mean. Just yesterday we got together for Auntie C's 70th birthday. 6 of Dad's brothers and sisters were there, most of their kids and lots of their kids' kids. There is something so special about being with people you have known your whole life. Especially the cousins Mom, they were my first best friends. It is always so great to see them again, no matter how much time has passed since our last visit.

I never belly laugh as hard as I do when I am with Jessica, Mike and John Paul. We are as close as ever Mom, thanks to you and how you graciously hosted all of those "cousin weeks" when we were growing up. The fact that you had 6 – 8 extra kids here for a whole week, on purpose, blows my mind.

Remember that game we had? How there was a boy's tent and a girl's tent, and the whole plan of the night was to steal each other's "plans"? Of course they never really existed, but that's beside the point.

I laugh every time I remember how we, the smarty pants girls, put nettles in the hole the boys had found in our tent. About 1 in the morning all we heard was the boys writhing in pain. Of course a couple of days later we woke up and found they had thrown all of our underwear on the roof of the pig barn. Oh, such great memories. Thanks so much Mom for putting up with all of us hell raisers. And I totally get it now – the mass chore chart. There's no way you could have kept up with everything without having us all pitch in.

Friends are just as important to me as ever too. I call – physically call friends on their birthday – not just send a message. Truthfully' actually, I usually do a quick video of me belting out some ridiculously bad version of happy birthday with a party hat on and send it to them. I know it makes them laugh and then I don't have to interrupt their day.

Also when somebody is going through some pretty heavy stuff in their life, I make a quiet note to check in with them. It means the world when you feel alone and realize you are not.

And the best thing of all, your 'second daughter' and I are as close as ever again. A very, very hard lesson to learn, letting a friendship die because of your pride. I can't believe I was such an ass to her.

That is when you know someone is a real friend Mom. We hadn't really spoken in 15 years, you left and three days later she showed up with an overnight bag and an endless supply of hugs. I am so blessed to have her in my life.

I never told you Mom, but once when she and I were "house watching" your parents' place and your Dad stopped by unexpectedly to check on it, well, we had two boys and a couple of cases of beer stashed in the closet. The closet RIGHT BESIDE the front door, where he stood and talked to us for five minutes. I know we did some sneaky things, but that one definitely takes the cake.

Okay, seeing as how I am getting out all my dirty laundry… One other time Mom, the only other time I told you a really big lie was when Ryan had just moved out downtown. You called me at his place, and he said I was in the shower. Well, I wasn't. I was actually at my boyfriend's apartment downtown. Ryan called me right away, I hopped in my Jetta and did about 140 km/hr to his place so I could be there when you "called back in ten minutes". Phew.

My anxiety stopped snowballing at the end of the Veg CSA the fall of 2016. There was no more watering late at night with a juice jug and a headlamp. No more worrying if somehow something had gotten onto the veggies and someone would die. Holy cow Mom, looking back I feel so ridiculous for the mess my head was in, but when I was in the thick of it, it all seemed so realistic.

I was still really busy with meetings but there were definitely bonuses to being so involved too. That fall the NFU sent me out west for a few days, and the food hub sent me to Toronto. I got to stay in hotels and have long hot showers whenever I wanted. AND I didn't have to cook anything or worry about taking care of anyone or anything.

I was still a bit anxious every day though, that hadn't gone away. Luckily it wasn't nearly as bad as it had been in the summer. The thing was, the second the garden was closed for the year I was already stressing about the next year even though it was months away. I had to do something, there was absolutely no way I would go through another year like the last.

I ignored the 'I should be growing vegetables because that is what I have always done and that is what people expect of me' idea. Businesses evolve, and grow with what works. The saddest part about the whole past season Mom was that I had carefully tracked all the time spent working in the garden. You know how much money I made per hour? Four bucks. Four fucking dollars an hour to lose my mind and let my family down. And that wasn't even including the over $1k we had spent on water. Nope.

In January 2017 I called Katie. She came over. I broke up with her. She completely understood. Mom I can't tell you the relief I felt, I could literally feel the millions of pounds lifting off my shoulders. It was the best I had felt in a really long time. And she was so great about it, of course as always. She didn't make me feel for one second that I had let her down. She is such a treasure.

I resigned from the Board of Directors of the food hub the following week. It was a really hard decision. It was such an amazing project and I was so proud to have been one of the founders, but all the meetings and emails – sometimes upwards of 15 a day surrounding it were draining my time and energy. Again, more weight lifted.

It was so freeing to step away from things that I didn't have time for. I had to re-organize my life and my time, putting me and our family first no matter what. I stopped doing most farm talks, farm tours, and anything that would feed Tom. Of course he wasn't gone altogether, but he was definitely shrinking. It was so good to finally be able to see the light at the end of the tunnel.

Everything started to get better after that. I slowly, slowly became me again. It was really weird to put on the brakes with the business, but I knew it was exactly what I needed to do. Yes, giving talks made a little money, but the trade-off of having no time, energy or sanity just wasn't worth it.

I really noticed it now, that whatever energy you put out, regardless of your intentions surrounding it, more of it comes into your life.

For example, the more I worried about anxiety - the more I got. When I decided to step back and concentrate on the family, all kinds of things would show up that made that easier. Things like more cottage invites, dinner dates and sleepovers keeping the kids happy.

I went to B.C. that winter, again so great to get away. I did my traditional Whistler visit and actually stayed with Cory which was a blast. The whole trip I was feeling pretty crappy but just assumed it was because I was so worn out from losing my mind the last few months. Went to the doctor a couple of days after I got back and turns out I had full blown bronchitis. This honestly was great, because I now had a good reason to sit my butt in bed. I had only had three days sick in bed in the last six years, and I absolutely love sick days. Guilt free laziness. Perfect.

That winter was of course still hard on the farm, because, well, nature can be a real jerk and throw you curveballs. All in all though, it wasn't too bad. It was cold, but there weren't too many farm emergencies to stress me out. The kids were so much happier with me being around more and spending time with them. It was great to be back to the wonderful Mom I had worked so hard to become.

You hear how being a parent is the hardest job in the world, but you don't really get it until you become one yourself eh? You hear about the sleepless nights, the total exhaustion, and then there is what they don't tell you about Motherhood.

Nobody tells you about how after a couple of kids you pee a little every time you sneeze or cough. And how you have to buy padded bras to hide how you point both east and west when it's cold.

And how years of breastfeeding turns your once perky bosom into two saggy bananas. I remember changing once in front of one of the boys as babies. "I love your boobies Mom, they look like pancakes." Gee, thanks.

When the kids were small, just after you left, everything went sideways with parenting. Simple tasks like putting on shoes or finishing meals would turn into a massive battle. As soon as I figured out what worked best, they'd grow up more and everything would go sideways again. So I'd adapt, find a new way, then they'd go and grow up a little more and I'd have to change everything again.

I picked up a book a few years ago that really changed my parenting style – so much for the better. "How to talk so Kids will listen, and How to listen so Kids will talk". There were some main takeaways that still I still use today when I talk with the kids, and not just ours – anyone's.

When they were really young I learned to help them name their emotions. I needed to validate them, not disregard them. No one likes feeling like they're unheard, at any age. The first ones we worked on naming were frustration and disappointment.

Like when they were learning to tie their own shoes. That's a huge step for any kid. With the boys I had to learn to stop swooping in to fix it and tie them myself. When they started to get worked up I would say things like, "Boy I can see you are really trying and it is taking longer than you like. That must be very frustrating for you, and that's okay honey, keep trying, you'll get it." Of course the more they practiced, the sooner they mastered it, all by themselves. They learned that frustration is a part of life, its okay and it won't last forever.

Or if someone cancelled a play date and they were down in the dumps. I'd say, "I know how much you were looking forward to seeing your friend. You must be very disappointed that they can't come over now. Let's see if we can call them and set up another time soon." I would always try to teach them to feel whatever they were feeling, that nothing lasts forever, and you can make choices to move forward.

I learned to stop saying 'No' to them. Don't worry Mom, the answer would be no but I learned how to say it differently so they felt heard.

They'd ask to go... swimming for example. I'd say, "That's a great idea, we can't go today but let's look at the pool schedule and mark down when we could go next week."

Or if they wanted a freezie. "I know how much you love them and for sure you can have one, whatever colour you choose, but first we have to have dinner. Want to pick one out now and put it on top of the box so you can grab it right away when it's time?"

This one was a big one – not saying 'no' to them and working together to find a way they could get what they wanted (if it was reasonable) when the time was right. It taught them that what they wanted was important. Everyone likes to feel that.

I learned to give them a choice with things they didn't want to do. Do you want to wear the red boots or the blue boots? Either way they have to wear boots, but choice gave them a feeling of power.

Another book that we read that made a huge difference was 123 Magic. It's all about consequences and sticking to them. You tell them first what will happen when you get to three, so there are no surprises. It's their choice if they choose to let it get that far. You have to use a tone when counting that means business, a tone that any tired and frustrated parent has mastered.

The trick to picking consequences is to make sure they are reasonable. I remember once they were going nuts and needed to settle down, and Chris said if they didn't by the time he hit three, they would lose T.V. for a week. We always stay on the same side in front of the kids; they see us disagreeing and we're done for, but when he said that I had to jump in. A week with no T.V. would be a life sentence for me.

And speaking of books, I had started writing my book again. I had a spreadsheet of our story, along with five main points I wanted to keep circling back to, using us as an example. I bought a headset to help me get it out faster. It would type what I said as I spoke. It was $300 and worth every penny. I would sit for hours with the headset, and talk and talk. There was only one problem though Mom, and it was a big one.

I couldn't stand what I wrote. No matter how I tried to 'be myself' and speak how I normally would to a friend, it all just sounded like another boring interview. I kept working harder on it, trying to make it sound interesting but it wasn't working. I needed to step away from it for a bit, and come back when it was coming to me the way I wanted it to. I had read enough inspirational books by now, I knew the ones that really sunk in. They were always the ones that were far more personal than instructional. I just had to find a way to do that too.

I was absolutely thrilled about the spring and summer just around the corner. There was absolutely no pressure on me, no nagging voice reminding me of what could happen. That upcoming summer we would spend as much time as we could as a family, and get away as often as we liked. I loved the one week vacations, but it just wasn't enough of a break. That winter I started planning mini-vacations instead - with us going away for a couple of nights every couple of weeks.

That winter was a complete turnaround from months before. I was back to where seeing the rainbow came easily, and thinking positive was no longer work. I was sleeping well, eating well and feeling great. I was me again. Awesome. Churchill said it best – "Success consists of going from failure to failure without loss of enthusiasm." I had refused to give up in the hardest times, and was coming out with a smile on the other side.

Chapter 12

"A day without laughter is a day wasted."

\- Charlie Chaplin

Here, Hold This For Me

I was so thrilled when the spring of 2017 came Mom. We would only have a small garden for our family, and the relief that came with that was incredible. We didn't have any huge building plans that summer, which felt like the first time in forever. The whiteboard had some white on it again. It felt like we were finally crossing the finish line with everything we had said in the beginning we were going to do. It felt so amazing.

By now we had quite the array of fun stuff for the kids to do – all things unplugged. Things like a pogo stick, a zip line, a trampoline, bow and arrow, slingshots. Again, so great to make the same kind of memories with them that I have from growing up here, even the messy ones.

I remember one spring day, when they were really young, I left them alone in the backyard, playing in a little mud hole they had found. I came out two minutes later and found them buried in mud up to their waist! Apparently the little mud puddle was really a sinkhole that just needed a little encouragement with a shovel and the hose they grabbed. They were covered head to toe and had a lovely array of mud patties to offer me for a snack. Amazing how in just two minutes kids can get so filthy. I never cared about how dirty they got though, it always washes off. I want them stained with the happy memories.

We welcomed a guy from Belgium that spring. He had his own car, which was such a change from hosting people who didn't. All of a sudden the pressure to make sure I was being the perfect Canadian hostess was gone. It was also nice to have a male as a helper for a change; I know Chris and the boys really liked it too. He was a really interesting person, and we had some great talks - deep talks. I love people who can be philosophical.

He and I planted the garden for our family, which was not even a tenth of the size we had been using for the CSA. We put down the past year's black plastic over the rest of the garden, and planted only pumpkins and potatoes in it. The pumpkins we would just sell at the road side for Halloween carving – not for eating so that took away any "what if's" Tom had, and the potatoes would feed us until spring. Finally I was enjoying gardening again. I guess I hadn't realized how much I had begun to resent it. It felt great to finally be able to go into it without a growing knot in my stomach.

One of his last weekend's here (he was only here for a month); some of his friends came to visit him. He had five people come; one from Quebec, one from England, two from France and one from Spain. They were all a ton of fun.

We all decided to play a proper game of baseball, seeing as how we finally had enough players to get a real game going. Of course the kids were the stars of the game. It was neat because the guy from Spain had never even heard of it and thought it was the best game ever. We all had a great weekend; playing sports, enjoying poutine and swimming in the pool. The kids loved hearing the different accents and learning about all of their different countries. Their own private geography lesson at our picnic table.

After the baseball weekend our Belgian helper left to continue travelling Canada, and one of our previous helpers, who loved Canada so much they decided to stay, came by for a visit. She and I had become very close and she often dropped by as she lived only twenty minutes away. It was so great to see her again. We get along really well, as if we were childhood friends. She's in my handful of best friends for sure.

Somehow that night I had the house to myself, which never happened. The kids were at a sleepover, and Chris was enjoying a well-deserved night out with his buddies. She and I had a few drinks, well, more than a few and I was joking with her how nice it was to have nothing to have to do with the animals. She had always gotten a bit squirmy around cats which had been hilarious to watch when she was staying with us. Figures; now of course with her return visit, the cats were all around her to say welcome back.

Molly, our female tabby was walking around making a really weird noise. It was one that I had heard before. I felt her belly, and yes, there was a tiny little nugget in there. We hadn't had her fixed as we wanted to have a litter of kittens for the kids, but thought she hadn't yet found a boyfriend as her belly hadn't changed one bit. But hearing that "meow" Mom, I knew what was about to happen. We had so many kittens here growing up; I know exactly what that certain sound means.

She jumped up on the counter and went down under the kitchen window, so now she was underneath the shelves that were under the sink. She let out a hell of a meow and I knew she had just had a kitten. Holy crap! This wasn't my plan at all for the night.

I couldn't get to her, so I ran like stink (somewhat crookedly as we were well into happy hour) and got the drill from the pig barn. I took apart the bottom of the cupboard so I could get to her, but still I couldn't reach her. I had to take out the dishwasher a few feet away, and dismantle more of the cupboards before I could get near her. I grabbed a hockey stick and very carefully swept her and the baby out from under the sink.

The cord was still attached. I had my friend hand me scissors, eyes wide at the whole ordeal. The whole thing only took about three minutes from when I got the drill to when I was holding the kitten, but it seemed a lifetime. The kitchen was now a complete mess with all the surprise construction.

She and I became a doctor and nurse operation. I told her what tools I needed and she got them for me. I cleaned off the baby with a towel and cut the cord. I then nonchalantly asked her to hold something. She stuck out her hand and I *almost* plopped the placenta into it. She realized what it was, shrieked and pulled her hand back as if she had been electrocuted. It was pretty funny, at least I thought so.

I ran and brought down the wooden box from the attic that we had all those litters in growing up, and set up Mom and babe in their new home. I got him nursing right away. So much easier with a kitten than a cow. We named him Griffin.

There were a few other babies here at that time too. With my anxiety to a minimum now, I wanted to get the kids involved once again with all of the animals. I wanted them to have the responsibility of raising their own animals. We got four wee lambs from Katie, just a few weeks old and needing to be bottle fed. The boys named them Luke, Anakin, Brian and Phil.

The boys were so good Mom, every morning and night mixing up the powdered milk. Watching them through the window, walk down to the barn together with the bottles; I'd have those parent moments where you heart physically hurts because you love them so much. Love is such a good thing.

We put the lambs in the big empty stall in the pig barn, with a huge area fenced off out front on the lawn so they could run around and graze whenever they wanted. Baby lambs are pretty damn cute, chasing each other and doing crazy leaps sideways out of nowhere.

It soon got to be a pain when we had to keep moving the fence to cut the grass, so I set it up out the back side of the barn. Do you think they could learn to turn around and go out the back instead? Nope. They just stood at the door, looking forward and baahed their little sheepy heads off whenever they saw us.

All in all they were fun, it was a great lesson in responsibility for the boys, but I think we were all pretty happy when they went to freezer camp later that summer.

Calving went off without a hitch that spring, everybody was born and alive and we didn't have to intervene with anybody. One morning we even went out to find twins – both nursing at the same time. What a beautiful sight to see Mom, and such a relief. Turns out though, when you have a boy and a girl twin, there's something like an 80% chance the female will be sterile. I guess the testosterone somehow transfers over in the womb. Oh well, at least we had another cow to send to the spa, even if we couldn't use her for breeding.

That spring we had a calf that needed antibiotics after bacteria got in her navel post birth and she became septic. The constant rain, melting packed snow and a winter's worth of thawing cow poo had turned their winter yard into a messy, muddy nightmare. Every step we took had to be carefully choreographed so you wouldn't lose your boot or your balance.

We got both Mom and calf in the barn. I was on the field side of the 16' gate and was carefully but quickly walking behind it, swinging it closed when the calf bolted and got out. For some reason it was missing a metal section in the middle, leaving a big hole. Momma decided her 1500 lbs. could easily fly through that hole if she came at it full speed.

I hadn't yet locked the gate and could see what was about to happen. If I didn't react, she would smash into the gate which would fly open and take me down like a domino. I had to do something.

I closed my eyes and mouth and dove into the muck at lightning speed. No sooner had my body hit the ground then I felt the breeze of the gate and the cow pass above me. I was alive, but now half buried in manure. Crappy. I stood up; my one side completely covered and looked at Chris. He held a blank stare and didn't say a word. Smart man.

I started down the field to catch the calf yet again. I got about 30 feet away and he burst into laughter. I was still too angry to smile but could see the humour in it. We got the baby her medicine and saved her life.

Our new helpers arrived midsummer. It's funny Mom, it just proved to me once again that whatever energy you put out, whatever your thoughts are, is what you bring into your life. When I had begun looking for helpers that spring I had a very clear image of what I wanted - a couple in their early thirties, and that is exactly what showed up for us. .

They were from Brazil and happy to teach us some Portuguese. On the fridge we put up a few simple phrases that our family could learn and say to them. It was so neat to see how easily picking up a new language came to the kids, after only a couple of days they knew the sentences from memory.

You'd be proud of me Mom; the importance you placed on table manners was definitely not lost on me. The boys now, finally, after a few years of drilling it into them, know they can't even think of leaving the table without saying "Thank you for dinner and May I please be excused?" Makes me so proud when they do it when we have guests over for dinner, especially other parents.

We have always gone to a Chinese buffet in Kanata for "Your" dinner on December 16th. I never know what to call that day, so I always just told the boys it was the day we celebrate Gramma. Now that they are older they understand. Lots of free surprise hugs for me that day, I love it. They look forward to it every year, knowing they are allowed to stuff their faces with French fries and Jell–O.

One of the first years we went to the Buffet, when they were really young, I found them walking around with their plates after everyone was done. When I asked them what they were doing, they said they were looking for the dishwasher. Bless their hearts.

Everyone we had hosted so far had brought us a gift from their home country and the Brazilians were no different, but they definitely went above and beyond. They were paragliders back home, and he had started making a clothing line with material from the used sails. They had brought both Chris and I each a beautiful coat, they had hand made just for us, as well as flip flops for the whole family. I mean seriously Mom, how nice is that?

They were a ton of fun, and we definitely had lots of laughs together. It was great to host two people that knew each other and I didn't have to worry about if they were driving each other nuts in the trailer.

A few days after they got here I got a short text from Uncle J. He had some tickets to a U2 concert but couldn't make it – did I want them? Me? Does a bear poop in the woods? Turns out it was in Toronto in two days – no problemo. The Brazilian lady and I headed off on our road trip. She had a daughter who was 16 at the time and Mom, it was so nice to have another Mom entrepreneur to talk with, and who understood the stresses of balancing a family and running your own business.

The concert was amazing, of course, and we had arranged to stay at Kevin's place close by that night. He was then in his second year at University of Toronto, and totally kicking butt in school to put it modestly. He is one smart cookie Mom, you would be so proud of him, I know you always were.

It was pretty funny stumbling into his apartment at one in the morning, trying not to giggle too loudly. He had to work in the morning so we quietly crept into our sleeping bags and went to sleep. Talk about a role reversal.

Our next worker was from Orleans but I hired her when she was in Thailand, so it still kind of had the travelling feel, right? I remember our first Skype interview. It was morning here, but late at night there. I got to the part about letting her know that we drank beer the odd time and did she have a problem with it? She laughed and said absolutely not, and then leaned out of the screen for a second as she said she didn't mind the odd drink herself. She came back into view with the biggest goblet of red wine I had ever seen. She was hired in that instant.

This woman was absolutely amazing and we hit it off right away. I went to pick her up in Ottawa, first time ever I didn't have to go to Montreal for a helper. In my usual twit style I couldn't be bothered to drive around the block again when I missed the street, so I quickly turned down a one way the wrong way and parked on the sidewalk.

Ten minutes into our drive I was in stitches. She wasn't just funny, she was downright hilarious Mom. She also had a very deep spiritual side to her which led to some pretty amazing conversations during her stay here. She had bought a car as planned a week after she arrived, so once again the tour guide pressure was lifted.

That summer my only concrete plans were to spend as much time together as a family as we could – OFF the farm. I knew the only way to give them my full attention was to be far away from work. Every couple of weeks we headed off camping with friends, or to a cottage. The whole summer it seemed like no sooner had we unpacked than we were loading up the truck to head off again. It made my travelling feet very happy.

By fall our summer getaways were winding down. The kids were now back in school – YAHOO!! Love them dearly Mom, but holy cow trying to work from home with them, well let's just say by September I really needed to miss them.

With them away I could spend some time working on the house. We hadn't done a thing to the attic or basement since we had moved in. It was pretty quick Mom, Dad was in Cape Breton when we decided to buy the farm after all, and we moved in that week. We put most of the stuff from the farmhouse in the attic and brought all of his personals to the round house for him.

All our stuff that we had moved here from our old place we had just thrown in the attic too. I would go up there and it would drive me nuts, so much stuff everywhere. Now I had the time to go through it all. Our Orleans helper and I tackled the huge job, and wow, what a difference. We organized Dad's stuff much better, and got rid of a ton of our stuff. It felt so good to be purging. I had gotten pretty good about letting go of things no longer useful in my head that season, and getting rid of the clutter was just as therapeutic. I know clutter drove you nuts too Mom.

I had completely given up on creating an app by this point. I had been working with a software engineer and it was getting too complicated with the hundreds of variables that would have had to be included. I had spent a ton of time on it in the past couple of years, but just had to let it go. It definitely helped improve how I would deliver all of the information in my workshops though, so that was time well spent in some ways.

I decided to go back to writing the book at full speed. I had written about seven chapters by that point, but it just wasn't coming out anymore. And when I read what I had written, it all just sounded like I was trying to impress someone. Nope. Down it went again.

It wasn't that what I was writing about was boring, but it was the way I was writing it. Here I was trying to write about how to just be yourself and know that that is good enough, and every time I would reread something, I kept changing it. I had to put it down. No way was I going to put out something I wasn't proud of.

Just because I wasn't writing it though didn't mean I couldn't be getting people interested in my writing style right? I started thinking ahead about what I could do to start getting people excited about my book. I started "blogging" and posting it on our social media pages. Basically Mom, blogging is when you write about anything – doesn't at all have to be about your business. It's a way of getting people to know you, the real you.

At first my blogs were horrible, long winded and empty. But with practice they got better and better. I studied my analytics and noticed people were paying attention to my blogs, often triple the amount of people would read them compared to anything else I posted. I also started getting lots of compliments on my writing too. It felt great, and deep, deep down I started believing that yes, I really could be a bestselling author. I just had to write the damn book, so I kept plugging away at it.

I realized by going back through all of my notes – I took notes whenever I read books – just how much I had learned. I wanted to put it all in the book, give all the best take-aways that I had learned and grown the most from. I just had to organize it all first, and then spit it out. That turned out to be just a teensy bit more time consuming than I thought, but I kept working at it. One foot in front of the other, you'll get there…

It's funny Mom, because when we started farming, we had so many plans and things we wanted to build and grow, the mountain of work seemed to reach the sky. By that summer, we had done it all, and then some.

I had a ton more free time not having the garden. All the fences, electricity and plumbing had been redone enough times by then that everything was running smoothly. It was so lovely to be able to breathe. And after a taste of heading off here and there all the past summer, I knew I wanted to keep that flavour in our life.

Most importantly I had grown so much Mom, more than I ever thought possible. Looking back I am so thankful for all that we have been through, the good and the bad. It all made me who I am today. I have such a completely different outlook on myself, on compassion, on others, on life - everything.

I realized last fall that I wanted to give more, somehow… We will keep farming of course, we love it, but there was a nagging in my gut that I was meant to add something to the mix.

I went back to the question you always taught me to begin with. What do I really want to do?

I want to help people change their thinking.

I want to make a real difference in people's lives.

I want to be able to work from any location.

I want to give incredible value.

I want to create something that feels limitless.

I want to always be improving what I'm offering.

Talk about clearly defined parameters eh?

Chapter 13

Right Into My Lady Parts

It has now been a full year and a half since I had almost completely lost my mind. I am so proud Mom, so stinkin' proud that I was able to pull myself out of it. Somehow I have moved past all the guilt of behaving the way I did towards the family, and Mom, there was a hell of a lot of it. I realized it was okay not to be okay. It feels great. It feels like a new beginning.

I couldn't wait for what lay ahead coming into 2018. I knew big changes were around the corner. I even started working out again right after New Year's. I knew I had two Spartan Races coming up this summer and I wanted to be in tip top shape. Sammy and Dana were always patient with me in past years, walking with me when I needed a break, but this year I wanted to keep up with them.

For four months I woke up at 5 a.m. most weekdays, did computer work until 7 and then get on my elliptical machine. I prefer running so much more, but after 10 years, my knees are done.

I would do 25 minutes of cardio while I listened to motivational videos on YouTube. A couple of times Mom, I was so pumped after my workouts, so much dopamine and adrenaline running through my veins, I felt like I could do ANYTHING. One time I was so overwhelmed with emotion, I burst into tears. Powerful.

They always say you have more energy the more you exercise, and is it ever true. Above all, it always clears my mind when I work out. After a few weeks of it, I had gotten back so much self-confidence, I felt unstoppable, and my belly shrunk a bit too which was great. Peanut butter cups had been a favourite coping strategy of mine the past year, and the resulting muffin top was getting just a wee bit too big for my liking.

I kicked ass in both races. I meant to keep training after the first one for the second, but I got lazy. No problem though, for some reason the second one, the harder one, seemed easier than last year. It was still really challenging, and so worth the feeling of accomplishment when we passed the finish line. Love the time I spend with those ladies. We always make it so meaningful.

Speaking of sports, the boys have been in soccer for five years now, and they are amazing athletes. One year William got Best Goalie and Charles got Best Defensive Player, we were / are so stinkin' proud of them both. The added bonus is that it's like a weekly play date for all the parents too. All you have to do is show up with a lawn chair.

They have won the end of year tournament every year since they began. Thing is though Mom, now they are called 'festivals' and not 'tournaments' with winners and losers, because someone's feelings might get hurt. BOO HOO! It's our job to get kids ready for the real world and guess what? Sometimes you win and sometimes you lose. Those that work harder get further ahead. That's real life.

This past winter was so much better than any of the others. The big snow blower that goes on the tractor bit the dust - finally. That thing was older than I am. We bought a new one, which was a ton of money but wow, it was like going from a Chevette to a Cadillac.

The boys were still having sleepovers here every weekend, usually with the same couple of kids. You learn pretty quickly the kids you do and don't want yours around. They have one friend who Chris and I like very much, and now we joke that he's our third son. He knows the drill, is always polite and happy to be kicked outside. It's almost weird now if he isn't here on the weekend. And when he's home, I mean over, the kids fight way less and head outside themselves more.

This past winter was pretty uneventful, but of course there was the odd adventure. One Friday morning during chores I found one of the automatic cow waterers had frozen solid. It made no sense; we hadn't ever had a problem with them. I took off the side panel and looked inside. Crap.

Apparently the heating element had fallen out of its metal sleeve, probably after the cows knocking the base for the last few years while getting a drink. It had caused a fire in the wiring, which luckily had put itself out, thank goodness. Can you imagine Mom if the fire had somehow sparked up the nearby straw? The whole barn would have gone up like matchsticks.

I took a photo of it, sent it to Chris and he picked up another element on the way home. We had just had a terrible blizzard, so he'd be working like a madman and wouldn't get to it for a day or two. No problem, we had another waterer they could use in the meantime.

Saturday, of course, just after the feed store closed the second one froze too. Murphy's Law eh? So now both waterers were frozen and the cows had nothing to drink. Crap. Chris, bless his heart fixed both waterers but it took forever to thaw the thick block of ice now sitting in both of them. Trip after trip he made with a boiling kettle, from the house to the barn, across the field through a foot of snow. And he never complained once. I was pretty darn proud of myself too, a year ago I would have been completely losing my mind that the water was broken, but this year I was cool as a cucumber.

We decided last minute to go to Mexico for a week at the end of March. The kids had never been on a plane and I couldn't wait to show them what it was all about - real travelling. Thankfully they didn't catch on when I had them try on new bathing suits and flip flops in the middle of winter. We kept the surprise from them until just three days before we left.

When we were on the beach down there I heard the lady next to us tell her friends about a book she was reading. She said a friend had written it, and she bought it because she wanted to support him. She said it was "One of those inspirational books, you know the kind, believe in yourself and blah blah blah." It stopped me dead in my tracks. That is exactly *not* the way I wanted someone to talk about my book – the blah blah blah part. I had to change something, big time.

I still haven't thought about what I can do to make that shift, to make it more personal somehow, but I will. I'll let you know how it goes, in my next letter.

We are now veterans at calving and were not nervous at all about all the babies to be born this past spring. When the Moms got close, we would put them in the barn so we could keep a close eye on them, often checking them every two hours. For our first calf this year, apparently that wasn't often enough.

I went out and found a newborn standing beside her Mom, who was lying down. As I got closer I realized the Mom had died. Her uterus was out of her about three feet, I guess her body had just kept pushing even after the calf was born. My heart sank. We had been so careful every year with calving, and this had never happened before.

I called a couple of close farmer friends and they assured me that this happens, and that with the shock it all would have been over quickly. It wasn't us and there was nothing we could have done.

Thank goodness for these friends Mom. I went to high school with Kim and Darryl and always really liked them, they are very genuine people. They have a farm a couple of roads over and have come to help us many times with castrating and ear-tagging. All of our kids get along well, and we've had many pizza nights and shared laughs over a game of cards. Very grateful for them, for so many reasons.

Back to the wee orphan calf. He was just standing there, not really knowing what to do. I don't think he even got to have one drink. I had to get him some milk, and quick. I went up to the feed store and bought some colostrum. Holy crap Mom, that stuff isn't cheap - $35 for one drink! He got a few drinks of it the first and second day and was soon thriving. Thank goodness. We named him Walter.

He definitely saw us as his parents, both Chris and I as we bottle fed him three times a day in the beginning. We'd let him out of the cow field for his meals in the backyard or garage and he'd run around with Stella and Blue just as if he was another dog. He was so cute Mom. He'd even stroll down the driveway with me to get the kids off the bus. There's that banjo in the background again eh? He soon became "Walter the cow dog."

Thankfully daily feedings after a couple of months went down from three to two. The nostalgia had definitely worn off after a couple of weeks, having to make sure to be home at 8, 2 and 8 every day as we didn't have a helper yet. He graduated from a bottle to a bucket, which I personally was so grateful for.

Remember when I was saying how calves will smash their heads up into the udder to get the milk down? Well if I wasn't careful how I was standing, or I wasn't fast enough in switching his bottles, he'd smash his head up for more – right into my lady parts. Occupational hazard. Good times.

We also had twins this past spring and called them Fred and Ginger. Walter was thrilled to have some wee babies his size to finally play with. We kept them in a pen with their Mom for a few days as it was rainy, crappy and cold outside.

One day I was working with the twins, and of course Walter was right nearby. He had to be anywhere I was, my furry 100 lb. toddler. The bull was in the barn too, so I was glad to be in a safe area in between the twins' pen and the main pen. Walter was in the big pen with the bull, mooing his head off trying to get pats from me. Then all of a sudden I heard a suckling sound.

I guess Walter had been watching the twins nurse and his instincts took over. I turned around and he was trying to nurse – from the bull!!! Juno didn't seem to mind, I dare say it looked like he was even enjoying it.

Walter would smash his head up into Juno's dingle berries, and then grab a mouthful of skin and try to get a drink. I fell right on my butt Mom I laughed so hard. After a few minutes the bull had had enough and walked away. Walter looked at me, crooked his head a bit sideways and definitely looked confused. Poor little gaffer.

The weather cleared and we let the twins out. We had a few more calves by then and they all loved playing together, especially at sunset – the witching hour. One day I went to feed Walter and he wasn't interested in the slightest; I didn't understand it. He looked healthy, wasn't losing any weight, was running around just like any other day but didn't want a drink.

I watched him like a hawk next day. You know what that little sneaker was doing Mom? He'd steal milk from the twins' Mom, going in between her back legs. Brilliant. The Mom was used to having two babies on her, so I guess she just assumed Walter was one of hers. I was so happy, no more milk replacer, and no more being stuck to the farm twice a day. It had been three months by then, and we needed a break.

One day later that spring started off just like any other. Had breakfast, nagged the kids till bus time, headed out for morning chores and that's when I noticed. The lawn in front of the cow barn was a swamp. I called Chris. "I need you home now." He was home 30 minutes later.

Thank goodness for great neighbours, Fred showed up with a backhoe right away to help us. We dug down six feet until we found the pipe. The ground was so wet that the sides kept caving in, and more water would pour in. Trying to find a leaky pipe in a hole that keeps filling with water faster than you can get it out is an exercise in total frustration. We finally got enough soil and water out and dried the pipe off enough that we could run and turn on the house pump again and look for leaks. At that exact moment, it started to rain. Perfect.

By this point Chris and I were both absolutely losing it, and getting short with each other. A shovel was thrown, and then my shoe fell off in the muck as I climbed up the ladder. I went to fling my other one in a hissy fit but it fell off before I could, so naturally I stomped like an angry toddler through the swamp in my sock feet back to the house. I soon returned with an apology and two coffees.

A couple of hours later the leak was fixed and all was well. We have had many catastrophes in farming and always solve them together, sometimes smiling, sometimes not so much. Trust me when I say sorting cattle, backing up a trailer together or fixing plumbing are the best way to test your marriage. And, of course, we passed. He balances me so well Mom. I am the drama queen, often overreacting and freaking out, and he's always the level headed one. Here's another perfect example…

This July was hot. Stupidly hot. We cut our hay the second week into it. Chris raked it over a few days later, ensuring it would be dry all the way through. It then got bailed without a problem. He came home one Wednesday, after his day of doing asphalt in 47 degrees (it was a terrible heat wave) and headed to the tractor. His plan was to load all the bales onto the wagon and tuck them away before Thursday night's rain.

And that's when it happened. He was at the furthest end of the field and a belt snapped, the air conditioning now broken. He drove all the way back in the tractor sauna. I went out to meet him at the barn, knowing something was amiss with his head now under the hood. He greeted me with a kiss and a hug and asked about my day. Now if I was in his shoes, I would have been cursing and completely losing my mind.

But not Chris. One of the many reasons he is so amazing. He takes everything in stride. He kept his cool and was as pleasant as always. He found the problem and headed off for a new belt.

I got home from deliveries at 8:30 p.m. He had fixed the tractor and was back at it, working until long after dark. When he did come in, he was smiling and joking just like any other day. Not sure what I did to get so fortunate, but believe you me, every day I count my lucky stars.

And of course, there is always the 'fun' with the cattle, giving me plenty of opportunities to be dramatic. One morning this past spring, Carlos the Cow had jumped a temporary electric fence into that thickly wooded area by the Sumacs, now carpeted with nettles and burdocks. No sweat, I'd lay a section of the fence on the ground and walk him out. The rest of the herd was far away, so they weren't any concern.

I get him walking out of the woods, he's 5 feet from where I need him to be when he pulls a U-turn and bolts into the thickest part of the brush, running like a 1200 lb. toddler on speed. So now I'm in 4 x 4 mode, chasing him around, and I keep tripping over fallen branches and getting a gazillion scratches everywhere. My legs are on fire with the nettle stings and I was covered in burrs. Sweat was dripping off my nose and I had to pee. Good times. And it was only 7:30 a.m.

I lost it. I screamed a word that rhymes with 'buck' no less than three times at the very top of my lungs, louder than even my Mom voice. I hear a gasp. I turn to see the kids standing at the gate nearby, their jaws on the ground. "Wow Mom, you're really mad." Yup.

Then I hear hooves, lots of them and they were getting louder. I turn and see the whole herd stampeding towards me. In a flash I grab some nearby branches and wave my arms in a crazy frenzy to stop them, which worked, thankfully. I quickly put the fence back up, but now I was screwed. I couldn't get Carlos out without letting them in.

New plan. I walk down the field, open a gate to a new pasture and the herd flies through it. Phew, they are dealt with and I am safe. I turn to make the trek back only to find Carlos right behind me. He was just casually strolling along to hook up with his buddies once again. I kid you not as he walked by me, our eyes met, and that exact moment he started pooing as he gave me a "Well that was fun" look. I had to smile. I love my life but wow, sometimes it's a real trip. As for Carlos, he'll be tasty eats someday but for now, what a troublemaker.

We welcomed another helper this spring, this time from Scotland. I had changed the job description by now, and he was happy to help with everything I needed help with, inside and outside the house. Also the plan this summer was to / is to go through the house top to bottom. I did three rooms last week and got rid of 6 garbage bags of clothes. It feels so good to get rid of stuff!

I am going through stuff as if we are moving, so when, not if (it's all about the language) the book gets finished and inspires millions of people around the world, we'll be able to build our new tiny dream house. We will have downsized enough, we'll be ready to move in right away. I have been planning the layout for years, all on my vision board.

Honestly Mom, that is the only thing I would like, that I don't already have. Our family is very close, full of love and laughter and you know me, I am not at all materialistic. I don't like stuff; I only want what I need. The one thing I would like though is a smaller house, one with insulation - that would be handy. Even with the woodstove blazing and the furnace cranked, that western wind still cuts through the walls like a knife.

And I mean absolutely no disrespect to the farmhouse Mom, I love the character and all the great stories it holds, but we haven't put a dime into it since we moved, and it needs quite a bit of work; the kind of work though that costs enough it would be a better idea to just start from scratch.

Speaking of starting from scratch, I now have an idea of what I would like to do, so I am working on how to grow the seed. It is so exciting to be starting something new Mom, the fire is again lit under my butt. I am now very comfortable being uncomfortable, so the thought of starting something new doesn't intimidate me one bit. I know its right because the past few weeks I keep finding myself jumping out of bed in the middle of the night to write down ideas, the possibilities are endless...

And speaking of possibilities, and how I have learned to change my 'lack mentality', why do I feel like I am being greedy wanting to have money? It's not that I want to be filthy rich Mom; I realize I already am, in so many ways. I only want what I need, and one thing I need is to have a more substantial secure income, and not be financially screwed by farming surprises. Case in point, I accidentally drove over a nail with the tractor this spring – it cost us $660 for a new tire. Grr.

I have to be completely honest too Mom, I am looking forward to not being known simply as 'the farmer', there's so much more to me, so much more I have to give. It's not that I want to be seen as some fancy princess with lipstick, high heels and perfectly coiffed hair, which definitely would never be me.

I am going on 26 years now Mom without owning a brush, I am still rockin' the finger comb with conditioner in the shower. Luckily I have great hair that doesn't need anything to look nice. I still to this day have never worn lipstick or coloured nail polish, and the last music I bought was a tape by Neil Young in the late 90's. I have never downloaded a song, and wouldn't have a clue how to, I don't even know if that is how you get music anymore. These dinosaur traits are totally fine with me, I have never been interested in keeping up with the times or the latest look.

And yes Mom, I still have those same insecurities about my body I did as a teen. I even blogged about it once, which took a ton of guts. This is how it read, word for word;

"I was born built like a brick shit house. I have disliked my shoulders and arms for as long as I can remember. They make me different. People always joke around and call them my "pipes" or "pythons", all in good fun but it still stings. Thank goodness I have big boobs and long eyelashes I can paint, both which help me feel more feminine.

While so many women work their butts off to build upper body strength, I have avoided weights like the plague. Throwing hay bales and lugging fence posts takes all kinds of muscles so they are useful, but a pain in other ways.

Every time I try on a pretty girl dress that should fit me snugly around the waist, I get it over my head and then hear the seams start to tear. Same goes for fitted coats, sweaters and T-shirts, very annoying. My best summer option is tank tops, which I despise because then I can't hide my arms at all. Going topless however is simply not an option, I was milked for three years and the ladies aren't where they once were.

Lately though, I have realized something. The only person who has a problem with my shoulders and arms is me. I am 43 years old and need to get the hell over it already. So I put on my big girl pants and wrote this blog. Please know I am not fishing for compliments in any way whatsoever, but to remind you that if your insecurities are holding you back from being the best you can be, you just have to learn to let it go."

Of course Mom, it was better received than any other piece I had ever written – because it was raw and real, just how you always taught me to be.

I have no idea Mom where my new idea will take me, but I can definitely tell it is the beginning of something amazing. It's like the last few years I have grown my wings, and now I'm ready to fly.

And speaking of flying, last Friday - September 21, 2018 a TORNADO hit the farm Mom! Chris, the kids and I made it to the basement in time, but the farm is pretty bad. Guess we have a little more work to do… I'll tell you all about it in my next letter.

Chapter 14

"Thank you for being everything I've dreamed

and a little bit more."

- Kenzie Lawson

In a Nutshell

Well Mom, that's pretty much it.

I can't say it enough how amazing Dad has been through it all. He was always there for me, regardless of how busy he was. I am so thankful for our friendship. He and I can talk about you now, in a way we never could before. It has helped me through more than I ever thought possible.

All the kids are doing well, and the best kids we could have asked for. Being a Mom now, I realize how lucky I was to have had the wonderful childhood I did. I see why you raised us the way you did, you were a parent when you had to be, and a friend when you could. It has made me such a better Mom, the only thing I really knew I ever wanted to be.

Chris has been my absolute rock. We just keep getting better and better. Life really is so good when you just don't sweat the small stuff and realize what's really important. I love that our love is as strong as yours and Dad's. We are one of the lucky ones for sure.

I can't believe how great it has been for me to write you this letter, so therapeutic. We have been through so much, and never given up. I am so proud of us. I never could have done it without all that you showed me about determination and perseverance.

You taught me my ABC's. You led by example.

Attitude is everything. Believe in yourself. Create your life.

I have learned to be uncomfortable, do what's right, trust my intuition, and choose to be with good people.

The biggest thing I have learned is that it's completely okay to be messed up. Everyone is, in one way or another. The point is to not drown in it, and think how you can make things better. The key is to love yourself, no matter what, and know you have the power to change anything. It's your choice.

There are no better building blocks you could have given me. Because of you I know the sky is the limit, and that I can do anything. I can't wait for what comes next for us. I'll write again soon and let you know.

For now, I love you. Thank you. *Cheers Mom.*

www.ingramcontent.com/pod-product-compliance
Lightning Source LLC
Chambersburg PA
CBHW022052050726
47591CB00002B/498